DAVE WINFIELD

3,000 and Counting

A Pioneer Book

Andrews and McMeel
A Universal Press Syndicate Company
Kansas City

A PIONEER BOOK published for the Minnesota Twins and Saint Paul Pioneer Press by Andrews and McMeel. Additional copies may be ordered by calling (800) 33-TWINS or (800) 642-6480.

Library of Congress Cataloging-in-Publication Data

Dave Winfield. 3,000 and counting / St. Paul Pioneer Press.
        p.   cm.
    ISBN 0-8362-8046-6 : $9.95
      1. Winfield, Dave, 1951- . 2. Baseball players—United States-
-Biography. 3. Batting (Baseball)   I. Pioneer Press Co. (Saint
Paul, Minn.) II. Title: Dave Winfield, 3,000 and counting.
GV865.W57D38 1993
796.357'092—dc20
[B]   93-36304
                                                 CIP

Editors:
Ken Doctor, Managing Editor/Features, Saint Paul Pioneer Press
Steve Rausch, Assistant Director of Media Relations, Minnesota Twins
Dave St. Peter, Communications Manager, Minnesota Twins
Lauri Treston, Deputy Visuals Editor/Design, Saint Paul Pioneer Press
Peter Weinberger, Visuals Editor, Saint Paul Pioneer Press

Contributing Editors:
Mario Casciano, Winfield Foundation
Wendie Erickson, Minnesota Twins

Contributing Writers:
Earl Bloom, Orange County Register
Jim Caple, Saint Paul Pioneer Press
Phil Collier, San Diego Union-Tribune
Moss Klein, Newark Star Ledger
Larry Millson, Toronto Globe and Mail

Dave Winfield 3,000 Hit Directory compiled by: Steve Rausch, Minnesota Twins Assistant Director of Media Relations, and Retrosheet, David W. Smith, President. (Retrosheet is a volunteer organization dedicated to the collection and computerization of play-by-play accounts of major-league games played prior to 1984. Most data from 1984 to the present was made available by The Baseball Workshop, Gary Gillette, President.)

Photo Acknowledgments: The Minnesota Twins, Saint Paul Pioneer Press, California Angels, New York Yankees, San Diego Padres, Toronto Blue Jays, University of Minnesota Athletic Department, Allsport, Bill Alkofer, Mario Casciano, John Cordes, John Doman, Gordy Jones, Charles Kochman, Ron Kuntz, V.J. Lovero, Ron McClendon, Buzz Magnuson, Rick Orndorf, Larry Stoudt, and the collection of Dave and Tonya Winfield.

Baseball cards reprinted courtesy of the Topps Company, Inc. All rights reserved.

Special Acknowledgments: Special thanks to Jay Alves, Dave Aust, Brian Bartow, Rob Butcher, Dan Ewald, Monique Giroux, Jon Greenberg, Richard Griffin, Jeff Klein, Jeff Idelson, Mark Leno, Tim Mead, Bob Miller, Jim Moorehead, Roger Riley, Glen Serra, Greg Shea, Dennis Smythe, Mike Swanson, Dean Vogelaar and Mario Ziino.

Additional Sources: The Milwaukee Brewers, National Baseball Hall of Fame, *The Baseball Encyclopedia* (Seventh Edition) and *The Ballplayers*.

FRONT COVER PHOTO: BILL ALKOFER/SAINT PAUL PIONEER PRESS
BACK COVER PHOTO: BUZZ MAGNUSON/SAINT PAUL PIONEER PRESS

Contents

The Winning Edge

BY JIM CAPLE
SAINT PAUL PIONEER PRESS

The journey to 3,000 hits begins with a step toward the batter's box ...

"You have to have a plan, the right attitude," Dave Winfield says. "I learned a long time ago you just don't go up there with your skill and past record. You have to go up there with an attitude. Everything I do — even walking up to the plate — is deliberate. It's not just a ritual without it; if I just went up and stood in the box, I wouldn't get the same results. I try to do anything to get an edge."

Twenty years and 3,000 hits. It all seems like it was so easy now. Too easy. Like he had an unfair advantage.

After all, wasn't Dave Winfield always the best athlete on the field? An athlete so good he was drafted in three sports?

"There wasn't a better all-around athlete in the last 20 years," says Bill Musselman, Winfield's basketball coach at the University of Minnesota. "You tell me it's Bo Jackson and I'll tell you that's a crock. When Bo was healthy he couldn't do what Dave did. ....You'd have to be a fool to say Bo is a better all-around athlete."

Surely Winfield's size gave him an advantage. Has anyone been a more imposing figure in the batter's box? He stands half a foot taller than Hank Aaron and weighs more than Babe Ruth did during most of his career. Think about pitching to a man standing 6' 6" and weighing 245 pounds. "Pitchers fear him," Chili Davis says. "Because they know he might hit a ball at them and end it all."

Jim Caple is the baseball writer for the Saint Paul Pioneer Press. Caple has covered Dave Winfield since he joined the Minnesota Twins prior to the 1993 season.

▲ Dave at the age of six — first grade.

Photo courtesy of Dave and Tonya Winfield

Has anyone hit the ball so hard, so often? "I used to hate playing third base against him," Paul Molitor says. "You just dreaded the few instances we would play the infield in against him and you had to play on the edge of the grass. Because he has the ability to hit a ball so hard that you would not have time to react to protect yourself."

Weren't even the planets and stars aligned for him? He was born the same day Bobby Thomson hit his famous home run, born just hours before The Shot Heard 'Round the World on Oct. 3, 1951. "And I have a good baseball name, too," he adds. "Win and Field. That's probably one of the best baseball names there is."

It all made it so simple, right? Just step into the box with that body and hit. So easy.

Of course, there was so much more to it than that. So much more.

Winfield is one of only 19 players in major-league history to reach 3,000 hits. But did the other 18 go through so much to get there? "Other than guys like Jackie Robinson or Curt Flood, I don't know of any ballplayer who had to go through the adversity I went through," Winfield says.

He went from college to the majors without a minor-league bus ride in between. He has taken batting practice everywhere from Mexico to Alaska, played on five teams, gone through 20 managerial changes and six owners and called more than 450 players teammate. He signed baseball's landmark contract, played for four last-place teams, 11 losing teams and didn't earn a World Series ring until his 19th season in the majors.

JOE ROSSI

◄ On September 16, 1993, Winfield singled off Dennis Eckersley to become the 19th player to reach 3,000 hits.

Bill Peterson on Winfield
Bill Peterson, Winfield's youth coach.

It has been almost 30 years since I first had the opportunity to become friends with Dave, his brother, Steve, and their mother, Arline. We share many wonderful memories that I will treasure forever. It is very rewarding to have been "Dave Winfield's coach." I know that many times I was given much more credit in his early development than I really deserved, but it was fun basking in those moments of glory anyway. I will acknowledge that I shared some fundamental skills with him that helped improve his baseball skills. Those fundamentals now seem so minute in comparison to what his family has given me and many others in return. From Arline and her sons I learned what true family love, respect and support was all about. She proved that when you self-sacrifice and give to others so they might grow tall and strong, that you grow taller and stronger yourself. Her sons showed me that the true measure of success and achievement is not what you gain for yourself, but what you help others to gain. And from David, I learned the most valuable lesson of all: If you believe you can, you can. Thanks for all the great memories, and now we have one more. Very few men have reached 3,000 hits, but somehow I bet Dave always knew he would. Some will say, "It would have been nice if Arline could have been here to see David reach this milestone." She is here. She did witness the milestone for her son, and she and Steve couldn't be happier.

▲ The Winfields: Dave and Steve, along with their mother, Arline.

▼ Dave posted a 19-4 career pitching mark for the Golden Gophers and still holds the school's career strikeout record.

Easy?

He has endured an ulcer and career-threatening back surgery, a trade and a release, strikes and lockouts, a bankrupt owner and a vindictive owner, lawsuits and counter-suits, and even an arrest for killing a seagull.

Easy?

"So often a gifted athlete is perceived as having been given all his talents. That he just wakes up in the morning and everything is there for him," says Toronto batting coach Larry Hisle. "I can guarantee you this, though. The reason Dave Winfield has achieved what he has is because he worked harder than everybody else."

Easy? It has been anything but.

"This is what I would like to say about him," Hisle says. "Whatever it takes to be successful, Dave Winfield does it. He does whatever is necessary."

Three thousand hits. Ten thousand at-bats. Twenty years. How many rounds of batting practice? How many swings in the cage? How many hours spent trying to get that swing just right?

"In New York I realized I would outlast my hitting coaches so I had video-tape made up so I could always have something to refer to when I was in a slump. The first four and half minutes were just of me talking to the camera about what I should be doing and thinking up there. That was followed by a highlight tape of me hitting the ball. It was like my greatest hits."

Winfield was a pitcher in college, and after he pitched the University of Minnesota to a seemingly safe six-run lead in the 1973 College World Series semifinal against Southern Cal, Gophers coach Dick Siebert moved him to left field. The Gophers needed just three outs to advance to the final, but they never got them. While Winfield watched from left field, Minnesota blew the lead and lost the game.

It would be a long time before Winfield got another chance at a championship.

A few days after the loss, Winfield decided baseball could provide him the longest career and signed with the San Diego Padres. He barely knew who they were. He soon learned more than he wanted.

The Padres had a losing record in all but one of the eight seasons Winfield played there, finished in last place three times and finished an average of 29 games out of first place. At one point, club owner Ray Kroc was so embarrassed by his

▲ Dave played a key role on the University of Minnesota's 1972 Big 10 title team.

team's play that he grabbed the public-address microphone and delivered this apology to a packed stadium: "Ladies and gentlemen, I suffer with you ... I've never seen such stupid baseball-playing in my life."

This apology came four games into the 1974 season.

The Padres were so financially strapped they had to sell a player to pay Winfield's signing bonus (about $90,000). They were run so poorly that the owner went bankrupt after Winfield's rookie season and sold the club to Kroc. Winfield once grew so frustrated he submitted a written proposal to the front-office personnel about what *they* could do to improve the team. How *they* could better run the club.

He was 24 when he did that.

Well, no one ever accused Winfield of a lack of confidence.

He was so young back then, and there was so much to learn. Yes, he had that great talent, but he had been primarily a pitcher in college. He didn't even bat his junior year. And that swing of his? Even Siebert said Winfield would never hit in the majors, that the hitch in his swing was too great to overcome. Suddenly he had to learn to hit without benefit of a day in the minors.

Winfield is a man who makes many notes to himself, and because the Padres didn't have ready access to videotape — these were pre-VCR days, when it was an event if a game was even televised — he took notes on a yellow legal pad. He watched team-mates, opponents, studying what they did to prepare for an at-bat. To those who had similar body types — Willie McCovey, for instance — he paid particular attention. Stances, swings, tendencies, even the walks to the plate, it all went down on the legal pad.

In Winfield's first full season in the majors, he hit 20 home runs. It wasn't long before they were saying he could win a triple crown. "They called me Secretariat," he says.

Three thousand hits. Ten thousand at-bats. Every time is the same. Every time he steps into the box, he vigorously clears the dirt from the box. Scrapes away the chalk. Digs in deep. Kicks out all that dirt. He has plowed more topsoil than International Harvester.

"What you see is what I feel and what I think. I walk up to the plate very confident and I display my inner feeling. I walk up with a swagger, and I clean out the box. I don't want to deal with anybody's remnants from their at-bat. I don't want to deal with anyone else's at-bat."

DOUGLAS M. MCWILLIAMS

He wasn't content to be just a baseball player, either.

No, Winfield might have been the finest athlete of his generation, but he always set his sights higher than that. He wanted to travel to exotic lands, meet as many people as possible. He wanted to be a businessman with a full investment portfolio. He wanted an appreciation of the arts, to be a fine photographer, an author. He wanted the whole renaissance thing. It was all part of the plan he had to live life to its fullest, to see how much there was beyond the St. Paul house where he grew up.

"Some people are satisfied with who they are as they grew up. They don't think they're anything else or can be anything else or aspire for anything else," Winfield says. "And it may be fine for them. I guess I was always up for a little bit of adventure."

"There's something deep inside him," Musselman says. "There's an urgent need to be more than just an athlete."

Winfield is ever the businessman. So much so, the man even keeps a fax machine in his home. And years ago when he looked at the riches Kroc had earned from founding McDonald's and establishing America's fast-food culture, he quickly decided this was something Dave Winfield should invest in as well. He didn't want to buy stock though. No, that would be too simple. Winfield's plans always fit his stature. He wanted to buy a McDonald's franchise. Kroc told him no.

Winfield now owns 18 Burger Kings in the Virginia-D.C. area. He employs 800.

Think about running a business of that proportion and still getting yourself ready to handle a Nolan Ryan fastball.

Winfield was one of the first players, if not the first, to make the briefcase a familiar piece of equipment in the clubhouse. Ex-teammate and manager Cito Gaston says Winfield will listen to music for a while on a team flight, "but pretty soon he's opening the briefcase and going to work."

Winfield remembers the generosity of his mother, Arline, the way she raised him and his brother, Steve, when their father

▼ Dave's senior picture, from St. Paul Central's class of 1969.

Steve Winfield on Winfield
Steve Winfield, Dave's brother.

I think playing professional baseball first became a goal for Dave when the Twins moved to Minnesota in 1961. I think it was then when we first realized that people can be paid for playing baseball. We thought "Wow, we gotta do that." From that time on playing in the majors was a dream for both of us. You hear a lot of people talk of David's natural ability, but Dave has always worked very hard to improve his game. Even as a kid, all he ever wanted to do was play baseball. He threw baseballs in the summer, snowballs in the winter and rocks in the fall. If you had to sum up Dave's career in one word, I think that word would be CONSISTENCY. If you look at his career, he has been one of the game's most consistent players. No, he has never hit 50 home runs, but he never hit fewer than 13 homers, either. I've gotten spoiled watching Dave play the game. I now expect 20 home run, 90-plus RBI seasons. I think one of the keys to Dave's incredible success is his attitude toward slumps. Dave doesn't believe in slumps; he believes in statistical adjustments. He has always believed that when the smoke clears his stats would be where they should be,. The fact that he focuses on the positive is a big part of his longevity.

PHOTO COURTESY OF DAVE AND TONYA WINFIELD

deserted them. How she always opened her door to whichever friend needed a place to sleep. He says it was that example that led him to begin the Winfield Foundation in 1977. While he can be very tight with his personal finances, over the years he has raised millions for the Foundation, and through it, thousands of kids have received free checkups, drug abuse awareness information, as well as tickets to games and plays.

It took time to do all this, but somehow, Winfield found it. Or made it.

"He'd come to a home game wearing a suit and tie and carrying a briefcase. And you'd wonder what businessman he talked to that day," says ex-teammate Gene Tenace. "But he was like Superman. He'd take the suit and tie off and he'd be a ballplayer and give you everything he had."

Winfield is as eager to give out financial advice as a batting tip. And when a young and self-admittedly untalented baseball fan asked this summer how to stay involved with the game, Winfield gave him this advice: work hard, invest well and then buy your own team.

Three thousand hits. Ten thousand at-bats. Each at-bat the same. Tug at the sleeve. Knock the dirt from the spikes. Slap the helmet. Swing the bat gently as if it were a pendulum. Stare at the pitcher, study the pitcher ...

"I'm doing a lot up there. You want to influence the pitcher. I need to go in there with my attitude. It's almost like I'm stalking the pitcher. 'I'm after you. I'm after you.' It's not, 'Oh, I'll see what I can accomplish here.' It's 'I'm after you. I'm coming after you. You're next.'"

Winfield's friends told him not to go to New York, not to sign with the Yankees. They warned him that the owner was trouble, but after all the losing in San Diego, by the time he became a free agent in 1980 it was hard for Winfield to see anything but New York's talent and George Steinbrenner's money. He so wanted to be a winner again that he ignored the warnings about Steinbrenner. Besides, he had never had a problem with anyone else, so he figured he would have no problem with Steinbrenner.

"Maybe I was a little naive," he says.

Winfield doesn't like talking about Steinbrenner, but occasionally feels compelled to do so. When he does, he rarely refers to Steinbrenner by name. He occasionally says "New York" as a catchall to cover all the turmoil he underwent as a Yankee.

The turmoil was considerable.

The problems began his first season, 1981. Winfield's famous 10-year contract, so lucrative he still was among baseball's highest-paid players when it expired, called for $3 million to be set aside for the Foundation over the course of the contract. Steinbrenner, he says, missed the payment on the first installment. "He said, 'If you don't like it, sue me.' I mean, I just got there!" Winfield says. "So by the next spring I had to (sue). On the streets if you cheat people out of $100 or $1,000, they'll kill you. You think I'm going to sit back and not take about $2.8 million (for the Foundation)? Yeah, right. We're going to fight."

That was the first fight. There were many more.

Steinbrenner had signed Winfield to be another Reggie, another Mr. October continuing the Yankees' dynasty. But after Winfield went 1 for 22 in the 1981 World Series and after the Yankees lost that series and didn't make it back, well, Steinbrenner seemed to hold those failures against Winfield. Forget that Winfield's numbers and play in New York were better than they were in San Diego, Steinbrenner still labeled him "Mr. May." The name stuck.

Steinbrenner also ignored court orders to make the payments to the Winfield Foundation. Steinbrenner also accused Winfield of misappropriating Foundation funds. Steinbrenner also hired Howard Spira to dig into Winfield's personal life, and, Winfield says, attempt to show he bet on baseball games.

"He tried to Pete Rose me," Winfield says.

Steinbrenner declines to answer specifics about his financial dealings with Winfield, but insists he never had a problem with Winfield the ballplayer or Winfield the man. He says his problems were with the Winfield Foundation. Eventually, Steinbrenner was suspended from baseball for his relationship with Spira.

Winfield started the Foundation to help people and continue his mother's generosity, but now it seemed that everyone was either questioning what he was doing with the money or asking him for more. Was life in St. Paul ever so difficult?

Three thousand hits. Ten thousand at-bats. Twenty years. How many pitchers has he seen? How many pitches? How many fastballs, curveballs, forkballs, sliders, changeups, knucklers, knuckle-curves, slurves ...

▲ Dave's aggressive play helped him earn All-American honors for the University of Minnesota in 1973.

Don Williams on Winfield

Don Williams, the San Diego Padres' scout who signed Dave to his first contract out of the University of Minnesota in 1973.

When I scouted Dave at the University of Minnesota, everyone knew he was a tremendous athlete; he could do it all. He had more natural physical ability than anyone I've ever scouted. In fact, most teams liked him more as a pitcher not because of his great arm, but because he was a rare five-tool player. The Padres wanted him to play every day. The thing I remember most about him, however, was the fact that he was an honest person. As the baseball draft approached, I needed to find out his intentions about his commitment to baseball, because we couldn't afford to waste our draft pick. He looked me in the eye and told me that he would choose baseball over basketball and football because he figured that the longevity was better in baseball. Once we drafted him, he went straight to the major leagues without playing a day in the minors, which was pretty unusual in those days. He struggled a bit at first, but Dave had a great makeup which allowed him to handle the pressure, and the rest is history. What sticks in my mind most about Dave is that once he puts on the uniform he has never cheated himself, his teammates or the fans; he's always given 100 percent. He has always been a leader by example; hustling, hitting and doing the job in the field, which every player respects.

No scout ever sees a player and projects him to reach 3,000 hits and to be a Hall of Famer, but it doesn't surprise me that Dave has reached that level. He has always taken care of himself and strived to make himself a better player. I can't say enough good things about Dave Winfield. A milestone like this couldn't happen to a better person.

▲ Twins General Manager Andy MacPhail presents Dave his 1992 Silver Slugger award.

◀ Dave and his mother, Arline, during the 1981 season.

▼ Dave and Steve celebrate the Blue Jays 1992 East Division title.

CHARLES KOCHMAN

Al Kaline on Winfield
Al Kaline, Detroit Tigers Hall of Fame outfielder and a member of the 3,000-hit club.

Dave Winfield is one of the best players that I've ever seen play. He has always been a 100 percent player, hustling every minute of the time that he's on the field. He is a great influence to the players around him. He's a surefire Hall of Famer. What a quality guy. He's one of my favorite players of all time to watch perform on the field. That's the way baseball is supposed to be played.

The Turners on Winfield
Louise and Robert Turner
Dave's mother-in-law and father-in-law.

David is a very personable, intelligent and energetic young man. He is keenly interested in his family and the young people of our nation. We do not consider him a son-in-law; to us he's one of our own. His marriage into our family has broadened the scope of our lives. We are privileged to share many magic moments together.

THE DAVID M. WINFIELD FOUNDATION

When the David M. Winfield Foundation was created in 1977, it was primarily a scholarship program and philanthropic organization for underprivileged youth. Like Dave Winfield's baseball career, though, the foundation has moved well beyond its modest beginnings.

In recent years, the foundation has taken on the additional concerns of substance abuse prevention, free health clinics, sports and fitness training, nutritional services and taking kids out to the ball game.

Winfield began the tax-exempt charitable organization while a member of the San Diego Padres, but it was after he signed his then-record 10-year contract with the New York Yankees in 1980 that the foundation became nationally prominent. Winfield specified that a portion of his Yankee salary go directly to the foundation's programs.

``When I was a young guy playing this game, I had a lot of time,

and a large earning capacity,'' says Winfield. ``But money is only part of my commitment. I've spent just as much in time and creativity. Over the years, we've done a whole lot not just in St. Paul, but across the country and out of the country.''

In its 17 years, the Winfield Foundation has spent more than $3 million on scholarships, medical and dental screening, computer literacy programs, tickets to sporting and cultural events and

furnished basketball courts and other fitness facilities to public parks in Minnesota and New Jersey.

It was in 1985 that the foundation took on perhaps its toughest challenge — the battle against youth drug abuse. Winfield's ``Turn It Around'' campaign initially conducted assemblies that reached some 70,000 high school students across the country, but foundation administrator Mario Casciano says Winfield realized the effort was not succeeding.

``He noticed the same kids out in the schoolyard after the assemblies getting high and asking him for his autograph,''

▼ Dave and Tonya dogsledding in Alaska.

PHOTO COURTESY OF DAVE AND TONYA WINFIELD

Casciano says. ``Since kids as young as 10 were beginning to experiment with drugs, he knew he'd have to reach them at an earlier age.''

So the foundation prepared the ``Turn It Around'' Substance Abuse Prevention Kit aimed at children in grades three through six. The kit includes an entertaining and informative video and activity book; the foundation also conducts training workshops for youth leaders.

In this age of multi-year, mega-dollar contracts for professional athletes, Winfield has shown the way for others to return some of their blessings to their communities.

``I've seen foundations emerge now that a lot of people are making a lot more money,'' says Winfield, ``and not just in baseball, but tennis, golf, football and basketball. Some have asked me for advice and guidance and I've helped to get them going.''

Casciano says Winfield hasn't eased off on his commitment to his foundation after 17 years of hard work.

``He can't,'' Casciano says. ``It's in him; it's his upbringing. He learned it from family, from his mom, from his community. A lot of people don't know this, but he was the first *active* athlete to create a foundation. His philosophy in life is that what you get out of it depends on what you put in.''

Steve Winfield, Dave's brother and vice president of the Winfield Foundation, also cited family upbringing for the philanthropic work the Winfields have done.

``Maybe because of the kind of giving, sharing person our mother was, it probably couldn't help but rub off on us,'' Steve says. ``Not only our mother raising us, but our grandmothers and the cousins and the aunts, the volunteer coaches, the mentors and the fathers.''

For 17 years, the Winfield Foundation's goal has been to repay the debt owed to those people by giving other kids some of the same opportunities and stepping stones.

PHOTO COURTESY OF MARIO CASCIANO

▲ Dave and Tonya at their 1988 wedding with longtime friend Don Baylor.

Roy Firestone on Winfield
Roy Firestone, Host of ESPN's "Up Close," and a longtime friend of Winfield's.

The only thing that exceeds Dave Winfield's considerable talent is his character. David Winfield is a dazzling athlete with gifts that are well chronicled. What should be equally important is Winfield's tireless commitment to his community. He is a magnificent human being. Three cheers for Winnie!

"People ask me why players don't swing at the first pitch more often. But there's a lot you can learn from the first pitch. How much does the pitcher's ball move? Is it sinking? Is it straight? Where's the location? What have their advance scouts seen? What is their plan to get you out? The more pitches you can have a pitcher throw to you in an at-bat, the better off you are. Because you've now geared your body and your mind to everything that is in his arsenal."

Usually one of the most engaging of players, Winfield grew guarded with the media in New York. One year he was diagnosed with an ulcer. Worse, at age 37 he missed the entire 1989 season after undergoing back surgery to correct a herniated disk. Some wondered whether he would play again.

Of course, Winfield did return the next season. But then Steinbrenner left his name off the All-Star ballot.

Winfield remembers taking a cruise in the Panama Canal Zone. He was talking with a group of tourists, laughing and having a good time when a crew member interrupted, telling Winfield there was a phone call for him.

"It's George!" the tourists sang out.

Winfield hated that. Hated how people always associated him with Steinbrenner. But as much as Winfield traveled, he could not distance himself from Steinbrenner, couldn't check that baggage at the counter. Not with Steinbrenner still signing his paychecks.

The solution, of course, was to get out of New York. And yet to leave New York would be to admit defeat. Winfield is as proud a man as you'll meet. He has his own game plan and letting someone else dictate to him is not a part of it.

"I always would think," he says, " 'here I am, not only a good baseball player, but a good citizen, an employer, a president of a foundation, a businessman. I'm not going to let you ruin my life. I'm not going to run.' "

Says Winfield's brother, Steve: "It was almost like he was standing up for what was right, almost to his own detriment."

So Winfield stood his ground, and in the end, Steinbrenner traded him to the Angels for pitcher Mike Witt in May 1990.

Winfield calls his seasons in California his decompression time. Freed of Steinbrenner, he found himself enjoying the game again. He could go to the ballpark and not have to answer questions about this lawsuit or that allegation. People asked questions about baseball or about his many other interests. He remembers a series of photos that ran in the newspaper that captured everything. The first showed him in San Diego, bright-eyed and eager. The next showed him in New York with such a scowl "I looked like a pirate." The third showed him in Anaheim with a smile and "a look of peace."

Still, there was something missing. The Angels had a losing record in 1990 and finished last in 1991. Winfield hit 28 home runs that year but to save money the Angels released him. He hit 28 home runs and people came up to him in the off-season asking, "Are you still playing?"

He hadn't traveled so far, worked so hard, practiced so much and endured so much only to go back to losing in obscurity in Southern California. It was time to step back into the spotlight. Time to show the world Dave Winfield was still alive and kicking.

RICK ORNDORF

16

◀ Dave leads a group of children as part of one of the Winfield Foundation's anti-drug programs.

PHOTO COURTESY OF DAVE AND TONYA WINFIELD

▲ Dave schools Michael Jordan on the finer points of basketball.

Bill Musselman on Winfield
Bill Musselman, University of Minnesota head basketball coach from 1971-75 who coached Dave from 1972-1973.

Dave Winfield is the greatest athlete I've seen in the last 25 years. He is the ultimate professional. As an all-around athlete, Dave's combination of speed and strength at 6-6, 230 pounds, separates him from the others. That overpowering combination could have made him an All-Pro in the National Football League. As a college basketball player, Dave Winfield was as good a rebounder as I have ever coached. When he went after a loose ball, guys would know to get the hell out of the way. He joined our club straight off the intramural courts and put himself on the line to help us win the 1972 Big Ten title, Minnesota's first in 35 years. I never had any doubt that David would be a great baseball player. Even when he was playing basketball, it was only after spending two hours practicing with the baseball team. But David wanted to be more than just a baseball player. He wanted to be a class guy. I was so happy to see him get a second chance at a World Series title in 1992. He rose to the occasion to help the Blue Jays just like he turned it up a notch at the University of Minnesota.

He signed with the Toronto Blue Jays that winter.

Three thousand hits. Ten thousand at-bats. How many slumps has he endured? How many times has he swung and missed? How many times has he expected one pitch and gotten another ...
"The key to hitting is finding an approach that enables you to stride into a pitched ball and attack the ball while maintaining control and balance of your body. Baseball's best hitters know that hitting is not guesswork. There are too many variables at this level."

Going to Toronto was like being reborn. After so many years of turmoil, so many years of losing, so many years of managers who he felt didn't stand up to the owner for him, Winfield was in an ideal situation. The club was the league's richest and best, the manager was an old roommate, and with the attention of two nations on him, Winfield had a great season — 26 home runs, 108 RBI.

More than that, Winfield became a fan favorite in Toronto. The city that once arrested him for accidentally killing a seagull with a warm-up throw now embraced him. When he turned 41 that year, a sold-out SkyDome crowd sang "Happy Birthday" to him. He had endured much on his big-league journey, but he finally found himself a hero again. He helped the Blue Jays to their first World Series, and in doing so, gave himself the chance for redemption. The only remaining stigma on his baseball career was the 1981 World Series. The 1 for 22.

Stepping into the box in the 11th inning of Game 6 for what would become the most important at-bat of his career, Winfield says he was able to think about the long journey from Minnesota, about the many years in San Diego and New York, the labels he endured after the 1981 series. About how he had prepared his entire life and criss-crossed the continent and worked so hard for this moment. About how he could end the labels and finally become a champion again

William C. Hayes on Winfield

William C. Hayes, Founder of the Chi Chi Rodriguez Youth Foundation for Abused Children.

As founder of the Chi Chi Rodriguez Youth Foundation and a professional golfer, I have met and been around many famous celebrities and athletes. Dave Winfield is a friend and a person who used his celebrity status to make it a better world for all people. As time goes on, and society faces critical growth problems, we need more people like Dave Winfield to make it a better world for all of us. He is truly a giant among men.

PHOTO COURTESY OF DAVE AND TONYA WINFIELD

▲ Dave and Tonya celebrate New Year's 1993 with Magic and Cookie Johnson.

doing what he had always done so well — drive in some runs. Then he uncoiled and swung at Charlie Leibrandt's pitch, bouncing a two-run double down the third-base line. The runs held up as the game-winners. Finally, Toronto and Winfield were champions.

Good-bye, Mr. May.

"The main thing people would tell me after we won it all is," Winfield says, "we're sorry our team didn't win, but if anybody deserved to win, it was you. We're happy for you and you deserved it."

Three thousand hits. Ten thousand at-bats. Four hundred fifty home runs. And how many more? He shows no sign of slowing down. He won't rule out playing after his contract with the Twins expires next year. Five hundred home runs is not beyond reason ...

"It's a real, real high to hit that baseball. People love to hit, even if they're not baseball players. They love to go to batting cages and stuff. It's a real thrill, a feeling of turning that projectile around, turning that horsehide around with a bat."

In his second at-bat as a Twin, he hit a ball into the left-field bleachers, trotted to first, circled second, rounded third and then David Mark Winfield came home.

It has been such a long and fruitful journey home and to 3,000 hits. He has traveled the world, seen the sun rise in Africa and set on the Himalayas, played baseball on the West Coast and the East Coast, played in the United States and Canada, met every sitting president since Gerald Ford, opened an art gallery, dined with Kirby Puckett and Wolfgang Puck, been arrested and given a hero's parade in the same foreign city. He is a 12-time All-Star, a seven-time Gold Glove winner, a certain Hall of Famer, a foundation president and the employer of hundreds.

Gone are the guarded days of New York. Winfield is quick to laugh, quicker to smile and quicker still to talk.

Winfield is happy. In addition to the championship ring and the 3,000 hits, he is finally getting to know his 11-year-old daughter, Shanel. After many years as a bachelor, he also has been happily married to Tonya Turner for five years. She recently gave him a set of paints so he can try his hand at *that*. The road to 3,000 hits was long and occasionally difficult. But it has taken him farther than he ever dreamed.

"It's too bad it took so long to win," he says. "I did everything an individual could do to be on a winning team, but I don't control the makeup of the team. There was nothing else I could do to prepare myself. I prepare myself correctly every spring but it didn't matter. If there's a lesson for young people to learn is that you don't always get what you want because you're ready. It takes time. You have to invest in yourself."

Funny how far a little hard work and practice can take a man. ◉

▼ Following spread: On top of the world! Dave leads the fans at the celebration for the 1992 World Champion Blue Jays.   CHARLES KOCHMAN

1973 • 1980

Youthful Triumph

BY PHIL COLLIER
SAN DIEGO UNION-TRIBUNE

You have to go back to those first eight seasons with the San Diego Padres to appreciate what Dave Winfield has accomplished since he left the University of Minnesota campus and went straight to the big leagues 20 years ago.

The fact that the 41-year-old outfielder/designated hitter has reached 3,000 career hits and more than 450 homers is made more remarkable by the fact that he joined the Padres fancying himself as a pitcher.

"I'll never forget the look on his face when he joined us in '73 and I told him he no longer was a pitcher," says former San Diego scouting director Bob Fontaine, who watched Winfield compile a 13-1 record during his final season with the Gophers, when he also batted over .400 as an outfielder and was named MVP of the College World Series.

"Dave had a great arm," Fontaine continues. "He could come in for one inning

Phil Collier is a baseball writer for the San Diego Union-Tribune. Collier covered Dave Winfield with the San Diego Padres from 1973-80.

and blow the ball by college hitters. But he was a one-pitch pitcher. All he had was the fastball. I told him: 'With your ability, you have to play every day.'"

Fontaine was but one of many scouts who recognized that Winfield had all five of the talents required of a superstar, meaning he could hit for an average, hit with power, run, field and throw.

Looking back, it is almost incomprehensible that Winfield was still available when it came time for the Padres to choose the fourth player available in the first round of the 1973 June draft. "I don't think I ever sweated so hard," Fontaine recalls. "The Texas Rangers had first choice. The Phillies were second and Milwaukee third. We knew the Brewers were going to take Robin Yount."

To the Padres' relief, the Rangers and Phillies passed up Winfield, and San Diego was able to select the St. Paul native. The Padres flew Winfield to San Diego with plans of signing him and sending him to play for the Class AA Texas League farm club Duke Snider was managing at Alexandria, La.

First, however, Padres president Buzzie Bavasi relented and let manager Don Zimmer take Winfield on a one-week trip the team was about to begin.

"We worked him out during the trip," Zimmer remembers, "and he hit drives in batting practice that looked like somebody hitting golf balls. We were going back home on Sunday night and I was worried that Winfield would be on a plane to Louisiana the next day.

"Buzzie called Monday morning and said Winfield was going to Alexandria. I said, 'No he isn't. He's playing left field for us

HIT PARADE

NO.	DATE	OPPONENT	HIT	PITCHER
1	6-19-73	Houston	1B	Jerry Reuss
2	6-20-73	Houston	1B	Jim York
3	6-21-73	Houston	1B	Ken Forsch
4	6-21-73	Houston	HR	Ken Forsch
5	6-21-73	Houston	1B	Ken Forsch
6	6-23-73	Atlanta (2)	1B	Jimmy Freeman
7	6-25-73	Los Angeles	1B	Claude Osteen
8	6-28-73	at Cincinnati	1B	Pedro Borbon
9	7-04-73	at Los Angeles	1B	Al Downing
10	7-04-73	at Los Angeles	1B	Al Downing
11	7-05-73	at Los Angeles	1B	Claude Osteen
12	7-05-73	at Los Angeles	1B	Claude Osteen
13	7-15-73	St. Louis	2B	Tom Murphy
14	7-20-73	at Pittsburgh (2)	1B	Jim Rooker
15	7-20-73	at Pittsburgh (2)	2B	Jim Rooker
16	7-29-73	Cincinnati (2)	1B	Roger Nelson
17	7-31-73	San Francisco	1B	Juan Marichal
18	8-03-73	at Atlanta	HR	Ron Schueler
19	8-12-73	Montreal (1)	1B	Steve Rogers
20	8-13-73	New York	1B	Jon Matlack
21	8-14-73	New York	1B	Jerry Koosman
22	8-14-73	New York	HR	John Strohmayer
23	8-24-73	at Montreal	3B	Balor Moore
24	8-27-73	at New York	1B	George Stone
25	8-28-73	at New York	2B	Jon Matlack
26	8-28-73	at New York	1B	Jon Matlack
27	8-29-73	at New York	1B	Jerry Koosman
28	8-31-73	Cincinnati	1B	Clay Carroll
29	9-02-73	Cincinnati	1B	Ross Grimsley
30	9-02-73	Cincinnati	1B	Ross Grimsley
31	9-07-73	at Los Angeles	1B	Claude Osteen
32	9-17-73	at Atlanta	1B	Carl Morton
33	9-19-73	at Houston (2)	1B	Doug Konieczny
34	9-19-73	at Houston (2)	1B	Doug Konieczny
35	9-21-73	at San Francisco (2)	1B	John D'Acquisto
36	9-22-73	at San Francisco	1B	Juan Marichal
37	9-28-73	Los Angeles	1B	Charlie Hough
38	9-28-73	Los Angeles	2B	Charlie Hough
39	9-29-73	Los Angeles	1B	Greg Shanahan
40	4-14-74	San Francisco	1B	Jim Barr
41	4-16-74	at Atlanta	1B	Danny Frisella
42	4-17-74	at Atlanta	HR	Carl Morton
43	4-18-74	at Atlanta	1B	Roric Harrison
44	4-18-74	at Atlanta	1B	Roric Harrison
45	4-18-74	at Atlanta	1B	Roric Harrison
46	4-19-74	at Cincinnati	1B	Jack Billingham
47	4-20-74	at Cincinnati	1B	Don Gullett
48	4-20-74	at Cincinnati	1B	Don Gullett
49	4-20-74	at Cincinnati	1B	Don Gullett
50	4-21-74	at Cincinnati (2)	1B	Clay Kirby
51	4-23-74	New York	1B	Jon Matlack
52	4-23-74	New York	2B	Jon Matlack
53	4-24-74	New York	1B	George Stone

◀ Dave's 118 RBI in 1979 led the National League.

NO.	DATE	OPPONENT	HIT	PITCHER
54	4-24-74	New York	HR	George Stone
55	4-26-74	Philadelphia	HR	Steve Carlton
56	4-30-74	Montreal	1B	Steve Renko
57	4-30-74	Montreal	1B	Steve Renko
58	5-01-74	Montreal	1B	Ernie McAnally
59	5-01-74	Montreal	2B	Don DeMola
60	5-05-74	at New York (1)	1B	Jerry Koosman
61	5-05-74	at New York (1)	HR	Jerry Koosman
62	5-05-74	at New York (2)	1B	Craig Swan
63	5-05-74	at New York (2)	1B	Bob Miller
64	5-06-74	at Philadelphia	1B	Dave Wallace
65	5-07-74	at Philadelphia	HR	Dave Wallace
66	5-12-74	Los Angeles	1B	Mike Marshall
67	5-12-74	Los Angeles	1B	Jim Brewer
68	5-13-74	Atlanta	2B	Roric Harrison
69	5-14-74	Atlanta	1B	Phil Niekro
70	5-14-74	Atlanta	HR	Phil Niekro
71	5-16-74	Atlanta	3B	Carl Morton
72	5-18-74	at San Francisco	2B	Jim Barr
73	5-19-74	at San Francisco (1)	1B	Mike Caldwell
74	5-19-74	at San Francisco (1)	1B	Mike Caldwell
75	5-19-74	at San Francisco (2)	2B	Tom Bradley
76	5-19-74	at San Francisco (2)	1B	Tom Bradley
77	5-20-74	at Houston	1B	Ken Forsch
78	5-21-74	at Houston	2B	Tom Griffin
79	5-22-74	at Houston	2B	Claude Osteen
80	6-02-74	at St. Louis	2B	John Curtis
81	6-06-74	Chicago	HR	Ken Frailing
82	6-06-74	Chicago	1B	Horacio Pina
83	6-07-74	St. Louis	HR	John Curtis
84	6-09-74	St. Louis	1B	Mike Garman
85	6-10-74	Pittsburgh	2B	Jim Rooker
86	6-10-74	Pittsburgh	HR	Ramon Hernandez
87	6-11-74	Pittsburgh	1B	Ken Brett
88	6-11-74	Pittsburgh	1B	Ken Brett
89	6-12-74	Pittsburgh	1B	Larry Demery
90	6-16-74	at Montreal	HR	Steve Renko
91	6-16-74	at Montreal	1B	Tom Walker
92	6-17-74	at Chicago	HR	Ken Frailing
93	6-17-74	at Chicago	1B	Steve Stone
94	6-18-74	at Chicago	1B	Bill Bonham
95	6-18-74	at Chicago	1B	Bill Bonham
96	6-18-74	at Chicago	1B	Ray Burris
97	6-28-74	Houston	2B	Claude Osteen
98	6-28-74	Houston	1B	Ken Forsch
99	6-29-74	Houston	1B	Tom Griffin
100	6-30-74	Houston (2)	1B	Dave A. Roberts
101	6-30-74	Houston (2)	1B	Dave A. Roberts
102	7-05-74	at Philadelphia	1B	Steve Carlton
103	7-09-74	at New York	1B	Jon Matlack
104	7-10-74	at New York	HR	Jerry Koosman
105	7-10-74	at New York	HR	Jerry Koosman
106	7-10-74	at New York	1B	Jerry Koosman
107	7-12-74	Montreal	2B	Ernie McAnally
108	7-12-74	Montreal	1B	John Montague
109	7-13-74	Montreal	1B	Steve Rogers
110	7-14-74	Montreal (1)	1B	Mike Torrez
111	7-16-74	Philadelphia	3B	Dick Ruthven
112	7-16-74	Philadelphia	HR	Jesus Hernaiz
113	7-17-74	Philadelphia	1B	Jim Lonborg
114	7-17-74	Philadelphia	1B	Ed Farmer
115	7-17-74	Philadelphia	1B	Mac Scarce
116	7-18-74	Philadelphia	HR	Steve Carlton
117	7-20-74	New York	1B	Jerry Koosman
118	7-21-74	New York	2B	Harry Parker
119	7-21-74	New York	1B	Bob Miller
120	7-31-74	Los Angeles	2B	Doug Rau
121	8-02-74	at Los Angeles	1B	Don Sutton
122	8-02-74	at Los Angeles	1B	Don Sutton
123	8-02-74	at Los Angeles	1B	Don Sutton
124	8-04-74	Cincinnati (1)	1B	Dick Baney
125	8-05-74	Atlanta	1B	Carl Morton
126	8-06-74	Atlanta	1B	Phil Niekro
127	8-09-74	at Pittsburgh	1B	Jim Rooker
128	8-09-74	at Pittsburgh	1B	Jim Rooker
129	8-10-74	at Pittsburgh	3B	John Morlan
130	8-11-74	at Pittsburgh	1B	Dock Ellis
131	8-11-74	at Pittsburgh	1B	Dock Ellis
132	8-12-74	at St. Louis	1B	John Curtis
133	8-12-74	at St. Louis	1B	John Curtis
134	8-13-74	at St. Louis	1B	Sonny Siebert
135	8-13-74	at St. Louis	2B	Sonny Siebert
136	8-14-74	at St. Louis	1B	Alan Foster
137	8-17-74	at Chicago	1B	Bill Bonham
138	8-17-74	at Chicago	1B	Bill Bonham

Dave made his first All-Star game appearance in 1977 and ▶
delivered the game-winning hit for the National League.

▲ The Padres made Dave their first choice (fourth overall) in the 1973 free-agent draft.
Paul Molitor (third overall in 1977) is the only University of Minnesota player to be drafted higher.

NO.	DATE	OPPONENT	HIT	PITCHER
139	8-17-74	at Chicago	HR	Oscar Zamora
140	8-18-74	at Chicago	1B	Steve Stone
141	8-18-74	at Chicago	1B	Steve Stone
142	8-21-74	at Montreal	1B	Dale Murray
143	8-23-74	Pittsburgh	1B	Jerry Reuss
144	8-25-74	Pittsburgh (1)	1B	Jim Rooker
145	8-25-74	Pittsburgh (2)	1B	Larry Demery
146	8 25-74	Pittsburgh (2)	1B	Larry Demery
147	8-27-74	St. Louis	HR	Bob Gibson
148	8-28-74	St. Louis	1B	Lynn McGlothen
149	8-28-74	St. Louis	1B	Lynn McGlothen
150	8-30-74	Chicago (1)	1B	Tom Dettore
151	8-30-74	Chicago (2)	1B	Steve Stone
152	9-01-74	Chicago	1B	Rick Reuschel
153	9-03-74	at Atlanta	1B	Tom House
154	9-04-74	at Atlanta	1B	Lew Krausse
155	9-04-74	at Atlanta	1B	Lew Krausse
156	9-06-74	at Houston	1B	J.R. Richard
157	9-06-74	at Houston	1B	J.R. Richard
158	9-06-74	at Houston	1B	Ken Forsch
159	9-07-74	at Houston	2B	Mike Cosgrove
160	9-14-74	Atlanta	1B	Carl Morton
161	9-16-74	Cincinnati	2B	Clay Kirby
162	9-17-74	Cincinnati	1B	Jack Billingham
163	9-17-74	Cincinnati	HR	Tom Hall
164	9-19-74	at Los Angeles	2B	Don Sutton
165	9-21-74	at Los Angeles	3B	Doug Rau
166	9-22-74	at Los Angeles	1B	Al Downing
167	9-25-74	San Francisco	1B	Mike Caldwell
168	9-26-74	Los Angeles	1B	Doug Rau
169	9-26-74	Los Angeles	HR	Mike Marshall
170	9-27-74	Los Angeles	HR	Don Sutton
171	10-2-74	at San Francisco	2B	John Montefusco
172	4-11-75	Cincinnati	2B	Fred Norman
173	4-13-75	Cincinnati	1B	Jack Billingham
174	4-14-75	at San Francisco	1B	Jim Barr
175	4-15-75	at San Francisco	1B	Mike Caldwell
176	4-16-75	at San Francisco	1B	John D'Acquisto
177	4-18-75	at Atlanta	1B	Ron Reed
178	4-18-75	at Atlanta	HR	Roric Harrison
179	4-19-75	at Atlanta	1B	Gary Gentry
180	4-19-75	at Atlanta	HR	Gary Gentry
181	4-20-75	at Atlanta	HR	Phil Niekro
182	4-21-75	at Houston	1B	Jim Crawford
183	4-21-75	at Houston	1B	Jim Crawford
184	4-23-75	Los Angeles	1B	Don Sutton
185	4-24-75	Los Angeles	2B	Rick Rhoden
186	4-24-75	Los Angeles	1B	Rick Rhoden
187	4-24-75	Los Angeles	HR	Rick Rhoden
188	4-24-75	Los Angeles	1B	Al Downing
189	4-26-75	Atlanta	HR	Carl Morton
190	4-26-75	Atlanta	1B	Carl Morton
191	4-27-75	Atlanta (1)	1B	Ron Reed
192	4-27-75	Atlanta (1)	1B	Ron Reed
193	4-27-75	Atlanta (2)	1B	Roric Harrison
194	4-28-75	Houston	HR	Dave A. Roberts
195	4-30-75	Houston	2B	Larry Dierker
196	5-02-75	at Los Angeles	1B	Don Sutton
197	5-04-75	at Los Angeles	1B	Burt Hooton
198	5-06-75	at Cincinnati	1B	Jack Billingham
199	5-06-75	at Cincinnati	1B	Jack Billingham
200	5-07-75	at Cincinnati	1B	Fred Norman
201	5-08-75	at Cincinnati	HR	Gary Nolan
202	5-08-75	at Cincinnati	1B	Gary Nolan
203	5-09-75	at Chicago	1B	Ray Burris
204	5-09-75	at Chicago	1B	Ray Burris
205	5-11-75	at Chicago	1B	Bill Bonham
206	5-11-75	at Chicago	1B	Bill Bonham
207	5-13-75	at Pittsburgh	1B	Jerry Reuss
208	5-14-75	at Pittsburgh	1B	Dock Ellis
209	5-14-75	at Pittsburgh	2B	Dock Ellis
210	5-16-75	Chicago	1B	Bill Bonham
211	5-19-75	St. Louis	1B	John Curtis
212	5-20-75	St. Louis	2B	Elias Sosa
213	5-20-75	St. Louis	HR	Elias Sosa
214	5-22-75	Pittsburgh	1B	Dave Giusti
215	5-24-75	Pittsburgh	HR	Jerry Reuss
216	5-24-75	Pittsburgh	1B	Jerry Reuss
217	5-26-75	at St. Louis	1B	Bob Gibson
218	5-26-75	at St. Louis	1B	Al Hrabosky
219	5-27-75	at St. Louis	1B	Bob Forsch
220	5-28-75	at St. Louis	1B	Lynn McGlothen
221	5-28-75	at St. Louis	1B	Lynn McGlothen
222	5-30-75	at New York	2B	Jerry Koosman
223	6-01-75	at New York	2B	Randy Tate

NO.	DATE	OPPONENT	HIT	PITCHER
224	6-01-75	at New York	2B	Rick Baldwin
225	6-03-75	at Philadelphia	3B	Jim Lonborg
226	6-08-75	at Montreal (1)	1B	Dave McNally
227	6-08-75	at Montreal (1)	1B	Dave McNally
228	6-08-75	at Montreal (1)	1B	Don Carrithers
229	6-08-75	at Montreal (2)	1B	Steve Rogers
230	6-08-75	at Montreal (2)	1B	Steve Rogers
231	6-09-75	Philadelphia	1B	Wayne Twitchell
232	6-09-75	Philadelphia	3B	Ron Schueler
233	6-12-75	Montreal	1B	Steve Rogers
234	6-24-75	San Francisco (1)	2B	Jim Barr
235	6-24-75	San Francisco (2)	2B	Tom Bradley
236	6-25-75	San Francisco	1B	Mike Caldwell
237	6-25-75	San Francisco	1B	Mike Caldwell
238	6-27-75	at Cincinnati	1B	Clay Carroll
239	6-30-75	at Los Angeles	1B	Andy Messersmith
240	7-01-75	at Los Angeles	1B	Jim Brewer
241	7-02-75	at Los Angeles	1B	Rick Rhoden
242	7-08-75	at Chicago	1B	Steve Stone
243	7-09-75	at Chicago	1B	Geoff Zahn
244	7-10-75	at Chicago	2B	Ray Burris
245	7-11-75	at Pittsburgh (1)	1B	Jim Rooker
246	7-11-75	at Pittsburgh (1)	1B	Jim Rooker
247	7-12-75	at Pittsburgh	2B	Ken Brett
248	7-12-75	at Pittsburgh	HR	Ken Brett
249	7-13-75	at Pittsburgh	1B	Larry Demery
250	7-17-75	Chicago	2B	Rick Reuschel
251	7-18-75	Chicago	1B	Ray Burris
252	7-18-75	Chicago	1B	Ray Burris
253	7-25-75	at Atlanta (1)	1B	Ray Sadecki
254	7-25-75	at Atlanta (2)	1B	Mike Thompson
255	7-26-75	at Atlanta	1B	Carl Morton
256	7-27-75	at Atlanta	1B	Bruce Dal Canton
257	7-29-75	at Houston	HR	Dave A. Roberts
258	7-29-75	at Houston	1B	Dave A. Roberts
259	7-30-75	at Houston	1B	Doug Konieczny
260	8-01-75	Atlanta	1B	Phil Niekro
261	8-02-75	Atlanta	1B	John Odom
262	8-02-75	Atlanta	1B	John Odom
263	8-02-75	Atlanta	1B	Mike Beard
264	8-05-75	Houston	1B	J.R. Richard
265	8-11-75	at New York	1B	George Stone
266	8-11-75	at New York	1B	Skip Lockwood
267	8-12-75	at New York	1B	Tom Seaver
268	8-13-75	at New York	1B	Randy Tate
269	8-13-75	at New York	1B	Tom Hall
270	8-15-75	at Philadelphia	2B	Dick Ruthven
271	8-16-75	at Philadelphia	HR	Larry Christenson
272	8-17-75	at Philadelphia	1B	Tom Underwood
273	8-17-75	at Philadelphia	1B	Gene Garber
274	8-18-75	at Montreal (1)	1B	Dan Warthen
275	8-18-75	at Montreal (2)	1B	Woodie Fryman
276	8-18-75	at Montreal (2)	1B	Woodie Fryman
277	8-18-75	at Montreal (2)	1B	Don DeMola
278	8-19-75	at Montreal	1B	Steve Rogers
279	8-22-75	Philadelphia	1B	Tom Underwood
280	8-22-75	Philadelphia	1B	Wayne Twitchell
281	8-23-75	Philadelphia	1B	Steve Carlton
282	8-23-75	Philadelphia	1B	Ron Schueler
283	8-24-75	Philadelphia (1)	HR	Dick Ruthven
284	8-24-75	Philadelphia (2)	1B	Jim Lonborg
285	8-24-75	Philadelphia (2)	1B	Tug McGraw
286	8-24-75	Philadelphia (2)	1B	Wayne Twitchell
287	8-26-75	New York	2B	Randy Tate
288	8-26-75	New York	1B	Randy Tate
289	8-28-75	Montreal	1B	Steve Rogers
290	8-31-75	Montreal	2B	Dan Warthen
291	9-01-75	at Cincinnati	2B	Pedro Borbon
292	9-01-75	at Cincinnati	1B	Pedro Borbon
293	9-02-75	at Cincinnati	HR	Don Gullett
294	9-04-75	at Atlanta	2B	Phil Niekro
295	9-05-75	at Houston	1B	Mike Cosgrove
296	9-05-75	at Houston	1B	Mike Cosgrove
297	9-06-75	at Houston	1B	Doug Konieczny
298	9-09-75	Cincinnati	2B	Tom Carroll
299	9-11-75	Atlanta	1B	Mike Beard
300	9-23-75	Los Angeles	2B	Al Downing
301	9-24-75	Los Angeles	1B	Doug Rau
302	9-25-75	San Francisco	1B	Mike Caldwell
303	9-25-75	San Francisco	1B	Mike Caldwell
304	9-25-75	San Francisco	HR	John D'Acquisto
305	9-26-75	San Francisco	1B	John Montefusco
306	9-27-75	San Francisco	1B	Rob Dressler
307	9-28-75	San Francisco	1B	Greg Minton
308	4-09-76	Atlanta	3B	Carl Morton

Dave stole a career-high 26 bases for the Padres in 1976. ▶

tonight. He's better than anybody we've got on this team.'"

Bavasi gave in only after Zimmer promised to find Winfield playing time without allowing the rookie to get in over his head. That first year, Winfield wasn't allowed to face certain right-hand pitchers he figured to struggle against.

The plan worked even better than anyone anticipated. Winfield took advantage of his opportunity by hitting safely in his first six major league games. By season's end, he had averaged .277, playing 56 games with three homers and 12 RBI in 141 at-bats.

"The day he joined the club, he belonged," says Dave Garcia, who coached for the Padres during their early years. "He was the first player I can ever remember being referred to as a phenom. I can't remember him ever embarrassing the Padres."

Well, that may not be exactly true. John McNamara, who became manager of the Padres in 1974, remembers Winfield touched off a beanball war in Los Angeles one night after he unwittingly stole a base with his team leading the Dodgers by nine runs.

▼ Dave hustles back into third base in a game against Houston at Jack Murphy Stadium.

NO.	DATE	OPPONENT	HIT	PITCHER
309	4-10-76	Atlanta	1B	Phil Niekro
310	4-13-76	at Los Angeles	HR	Stan Wall
311	4-14-76	at Los Angeles	HR	Don Sutton
312	4-14-76	at Los Angeles	1B	Mike Marshall
313	4-16-76	at Houston	1B	Joe Niekro
314	4-17-76	at Houston	2B	J.R. Richard
315	4-21-76	at Cincinnati	1B	Don Gullett
316	4-23-76	St. Louis	2B	John Denny
317	4-23-76	St. Louis	1B	John Denny
318	4-24-76	St. Louis	1B	Pete Falcone
319	4-26-76	Chicago	1B	Rick Reuschel
320	4-29-76	Chicago	1B	Mike Garman
321	5-01-76	Pittsburgh	1B	John Candelaria
322	5-01-76	Pittsburgh	1B	Bob Moose
323	5-02-76	Pittsburgh	1B	Dave Giusti
324	5-06-76	at Montreal	HR	Clay Kirby
325	5-06-76	at Montreal	1B	Clay Kirby
326	5-06-76	at Montreal	1B	Steve Renko
327	5-07-76	at New York	1B	Jerry Koosman
328	5-07-76	at New York	1B	Jerry Koosman
329	5-07-76	at New York	1B	Jerry Koosman
330	5-08-76	at New York	1B	Mickey Lolich
331	5-08-76	at New York	2B	Mickey Lolich
332	5-08-76	at New York	2B	Mickey Lolich
333	5-09-76	at New York	HR	Tom Seaver
334	5-11-76	at Philadelphia	2B	Steve Carlton
335	5-11-76	at Philadelphia	2B	Steve Carlton
336	5-14-76	at Chicago	1B	Paul Reuschel
337	5-14-76	at Chicago	1B	Paul Reuschel
338	5-14-76	at Chicago	1B	Mike Garman
339	5-16-76	at Chicago	1B	Rick Reuschel
340	5-16-76	at Chicago	2B	Rick Reuschel
341	5-17-76	at San Francisco	1B	Dave Heaverlo
342	5-18-76	at San Francisco	2B	Randy Moffitt
343	5-20-76	Houston	HR	Ken Forsch
344	5-21-76	Cincinnati	HR	Gary Nolan
345	5-22-76	Cincinnati	2B	Pat Zachry
346	5-27-76	San Francisco	1B	Ed Halicki
347	5-29-76	San Francisco	1B	Rob Dressler
348	5-29-76	San Francisco	1B	Dave Heaverlo
349	5-30-76	San Francisco	1B	Mike Caldwell
350	5-31-76	at Atlanta	HR	Max Leon
351	6-01-76	at Atlanta	1B	Roger Moret
352	6-04-76	at Pittsburgh	1B	Jerry Reuss
353	6-05-76	at Pittsburgh	1B	Doc Medich
354	6-05-76	at Pittsburgh	HR	Larry Demery
355	6-06-76	at Pittsburgh	1B	John Candelaria
356	6-06-76	at Pittsburgh	1B	John Candelaria
357	6-06-76	at Pittsburgh	2B	Larry Demery
358	6-07-76	New York	HR	Skip Lockwood
359	6-08-76	New York	1B	Rick Baldwin
360	6-09-76	New York	1B	Tom Seaver
361	6-11-76	Philadelphia	HR	Jim Kaat
362	6-12-76	Philadelphia	1B	Gene Garber
363	6-13-76	Philadelphia (1)	1B	Wayne Twitchell
364	6-14-76	Montreal	1B	Don Stanhouse
365	6-15-76	Montreal	2B	Don Carrithers
366	6-16-76	Montreal	1B	Dan Warthen
367	6-18-76	at St. Louis	HR	Pete Falcone
368	6-18-76	at St. Louis	1B	Pete Falcone
369	6-19-76	at St. Louis	1B	John Curtis
370	6-20-76	at St. Louis	2B	Bob Forsch
371	6-21-76	San Francisco	1B	John Montefusco
372	6-21-76	San Francisco	2B	John Montefusco
373	6-21-76	San Francisco	1B	Mike Caldwell
374	6-22-76	San Francisco	2B	John D'Acquisto
375	6-22-76	San Francisco	1B	John D'Acquisto
376	6-23-76	at San Francisco (1)	1B	Rob Dressler
377	6-23-76	at San Francisco (2)	1B	Jim Barr
378	6-23-76	at San Francisco (2)	1B	John Montefusco
379	6-24-76	at San Francisco	1B	Charlie Williams
380	6-26-76	Atlanta (2)	2B	Phil Niekro
381	6-26-76	Atlanta (2)	2B	Phil Niekro
382	6-28-76	Cincinnati	1B	Santo Alcala
383	6-28-76	Cincinnati	1B	Will McEnaney
384	6-29-76	Cincinnati	1B	Gary Nolan
385	6-29-76	Cincinnati	1B	Pedro Borbon
386	6-30-76	Cincinnati	1B	Jack Billingham
387	7-02-76	Los Angeles	1B	Don Sutton
388	7-04-76	at Los Angeles	HR	Tommy John
389	7-04-76	at Los Angeles	2B	Charlie Hough
390	7-04-76	at Los Angeles	2B	Stan Wall
391	7-05-76	at Chicago	1B	Steve Renko
392	7-06-76	at Chicago	1B	Steve Stone
393	7-06-76	at Chicago	1B	Rick Reuschel

Thousands of youngsters take in the action of a Padres game in the "Winfield Pavilion," compliments of Dave. ▼

NO.	DATE	OPPONENT	HIT	PITCHER
394	7-08-76	at Chicago	1B	Bill Bonham
395	7-08-76	at Chicago	1B	Bill Bonham
396	7-09-76	at Philadelphia	1B	Tom Underwood
397	7-10-76	at Philadelphia (1)	1B	Steve Carlton
398	7-10-76	at Philadelphia (2)	2B	Jim Lonborg
399	7-11-76	at Philadelphia	1B	Jim Kaat
400	7-15-76	St. Louis	1B	Bob Forsch
401	7-17-76	St. Louis	1B	John Denny
402	7-19-76	Chicago	1B	Bill Bonham
403	7-19-76	Chicago	3B	Bill Bonham
404	7-20-76	Philadelphia	3B	Steve Carlton
405	7-21-76	Philadelphia	1B	Jim Kaat
406	7-22-76	at Los Angeles	1B	Rick Rhoden
407	7-22-76	at Los Angeles	1B	Rick Rhoden
408	7-23-76	at Los Angeles	1B	Tommy John
409	7-24-76	Los Angeles	2B	Elias Sosa
410	7-25-76	Los Angeles	1B	Doug Rau
411	7-27-76	at Houston	1B	J.R. Richard
412	7-30-76	at Cincinnati (1)	1B	Don Gullett
413	7-30-76	at Cincinnati (2)	2B	Gary Nolan
414	8-02-76	at Atlanta (1)	1B	Bruce Dal Canton
415	8-02-76	at Atlanta (2)	1B	Bruce Dal Canton
416	8-02-76	at Atlanta (2)	1B	Max Leon
417	8-03-76	at Atlanta	1B	Andy Messersmith
418	8-03-76	at Atlanta	2B	Andy Messersmith
419	8-04-76	at Atlanta	1B	Dick Ruthven
420	8-04-76	at Atlanta	2B	Dick Ruthven
421	8-05-76	Houston	1B	Bo McLaughlin
422	8-10-76	at New York	HR	Jerry Koosman
423	8-12-76	at New York	1B	Tom Seaver
424	8-13-76	at Montreal (2)	3B	Steve Dunning
425	8-14-76	at Montreal	1B	Don Stanhouse
426	8-14-76	at Montreal	1B	Don Stanhouse
427	8-14-76	at Montreal	1B	Bob Lang
428	8-15-76	at Montreal	1B	Don Carrithers
429	8-15-76	at Montreal	1B	Dale Murray
430	8-16-76	at St. Louis	1B	Lynn McGlothen
431	8-17-76	at St. Louis	1B	John Denny
432	8-17-76	at St. Louis	1B	John Denny
433	8-18-76	at St. Louis	1B	Pete Falcone
434	8-21-76	New York	1B	Jerry Koosman
435	8-24-76	Pittsburgh	1B	John Candelaria
436	8-25-76	Pittsburgh	1B	Bruce Kison
437	8-27-76	Montreal	1B	Woodie Fryman
438	8-28-76	Montreal	2B	Chuck Taylor
439	8-31-76	at Pittsburgh	1B	Jerry Reuss
440	8-31-76	at Pittsburgh	1B	Jerry Reuss
441	9-03-76	at San Francisco	1B	Jim Barr
442	9-04-76	at San Francisco	2B	Ed Halicki
443	9-05-76	at San Francisco (1)	1B	John Montefusco
444	9-05-76	at San Francisco (1)	1B	John Montefusco
445	9-05-76	at San Francisco (2)	1B	Rob Dressler
446	9-06-76	at San Francisco (2)	1B	Charlie Williams
447	4-08-77	at Cincinnati	1B	Jack Billingham
448	4-08-77	at Cincinnati	1B	Jack Billingham
449	4-09-77	at Cincinnati	1B	Fred Norman
450	4-09-77	at Cincinnati	1B	Fred Norman
451	4-09-77	at Cincinnati	HR	Rawley Eastwick
452	4-10-77	at Cincinnati	2B	Santo Alcala
453	4-10-77	at Cincinnati	2B	Santo Alcala
454	4-10-77	at Cincinnati	1B	Dale Murray
455	4-15-77	Cincinnati	1B	Santo Alcala
456	4-15-77	Cincinnati	1B	Santo Alcala
457	4-16-77	Cincinnati	3B	Dale Murray
458	4-16-77	Cincinnati	2B	Rawley Eastwick
459	4-17-77	Cincinnati	1B	Pat Zachry
460	4-18-77	at Atlanta	1B	Frank LaCorte
461	4-18-77	at Atlanta	1B	Jamie Easterly
462	4-20-77	at Atlanta	2B	Andy Messersmith
463	4-20-77	at Atlanta	1B	Rick Camp
464	4-22-77	at Houston	1B	J.R. Richard
465	4-23-77	at Houston (1)	1B	Joaquin Andujar
466	4-23-77	at Houston (2)	1B	Floyd Bannister
467	4-24-77	at Houston	1B	Doug Konieczny
468	4-24-77	at Houston	1B	Joe Sambito
469	4-25-77	Los Angeles	HR	Rick Rhoden
470	4-25-77	Los Angeles	1B	Rick Rhoden
471	4-26-77	Los Angeles	1B	Don Sutton
472	4-27-77	Los Angeles	HR	Doug Rau
473	4-28-77	Los Angeles	1B	Burt Hooton
474	4-29-77	New York	HR	Jon Matlack
475	5-01-77	New York	1B	Craig Swan
476	5-01-77	New York	1B	Craig Swan
477	5-03-77	Philadelphia	1B	Steve Carlton
478	5-03-77	Philadelphia	1B	Steve Carlton

NO.	DATE	OPPONENT	HIT	PITCHER
479	5-04-77	Philadelphia	2B	Jim Kaat
480	5-04-77	Philadelphia	1B	Jim Kaat
481	5-05-77	Philadelphia	1B	Randy Lerch
482	5-05-77	Philadelphia	HR	Gene Garber
483	5-06-77	Montreal	1B	Jeff Terpko
484	5-07-77	Montreal	HR	Don Stanhouse
485	5-11-77	at New York (1)	HR	Tom Seaver
486	5-11-77	at New York (1)	1B	Bob Apodaca
487	5-11-77	at New York (1)	1B	Skip Lockwood
488	5-11-77	at New York (2)	1B	Craig Swan
489	5-12-77	at New York	1B	Jerry Koosman
490	5-12-77	at New York	3B	Bob Myrick
491	5-13-77	at Philadelphia	2B	Wayne Twitchell
492	5-13-77	at Philadelphia	1B	Warren Brusstar
493	5-14-77	at Philadelphia	2B	Jim Kaat
494	5-14-77	at Philadelphia	HR	Tom Underwood
495	5-15-77	at Philadelphia	2B	Steve Carlton
496	5-16-77	at Chicago	3B	Willie Hernandez
497	5-17-77	at Chicago	1B	Bill Bonham
498	5-19-77	at Montreal	1B	Don Stanhouse
499	5-20-77	at Montreal	1B	Jackie Brown
500	5-20-77	at Montreal	3B	Joe Kerrigan
501	5-21-77	at Montreal	HR	Dan Warthen
502	5-21-77	at Montreal	1B	Dan Warthen
503	5-21-77	at Montreal	2B	Joe Kerrigan
504	5-23-77	Atlanta	1B	Phil Niekro
505	5-25-77	Atlanta	HR	Jamie Easterly
506	5-27-77	Houston	1B	Bo McLaughlin
507	5-28-77	Houston	2B	Floyd Bannister
508	5-29-77	Houston	HR	Mark Lemongello
509	5-30-77	at San Francisco (1)	3B	Lynn McGlothen
510	5-30-77	at San Francisco (2)	1B	Dave Heaverlo
511	5-30-77	at San Francisco (2)	1B	Randy Moffitt
512	5-31-77	at San Francisco	1B	Jim Barr
513	6-01-77	at San Francisco	1B	Ed Halicki
514	6-03-77	at Los Angeles	2B	Don Sutton
515	6-03-77	at Los Angeles	HR	Charlie Hough
516	6-07-77	at St. Louis	HR	Buddy Schultz
517	6-07-77	at St. Louis	1B	John Urrea
518	6-08-77	at St. Louis	1B	Eric Rasmussen
519	6-10-77	at Pittsburgh	3B	Odell Jones
520	6-11-77	at Pittsburgh	HR	John Candelaria
521	6-12-77	at Pittsburgh (1)	2B	Jerry Reuss
522	6-14-77	Chicago	1B	Bill Bonham
523	6-15-77	Chicago	1B	Rick Reuschel
524	6-16-77	Chicago	1B	Ray Burris
525	6-17-77	St. Louis	1B	John Denny
526	6-18-77	St. Louis	1B	Rawley Eastwick
527	6-19-77	St. Louis	1B	Bob Forsch
528	6-19-77	St. Louis	HR	Bob Forsch
529	6-20-77	Pittsburgh	1B	Odell Jones
530	6-21-77	Pittsburgh	1B	John Candelaria
531	6-22-77	Pittsburgh	1B	Jerry Reuss
532	6-22-77	Pittsburgh	1B	Jerry Reuss
533	6-24-77	at Atlanta	HR	Steve Hargan
534	6-24-77	at Atlanta	1B	Dave Campbell
535	6-25-77	at Atlanta	1B	Andy Messersmith
536	6-25-77	at Atlanta	1B	Andy Messersmith
537	6-25-77	at Atlanta	2B	Rick Camp
538	6-25-77	at Atlanta	HR	Dave Campbell
539	6-26-77	at Atlanta	1B	Phil Niekro
540	6-27-77	at Houston	1B	Floyd Bannister
541	6-27-77	at Houston	HR	Gene Pentz
542	6-29-77	at Houston	1B	Dan Larson
543	7-03-77	Cincinnati	1B	Jack Billingham
544	7-05-77	Houston	HR	Dan Larson
545	7-05-77	Houston	1B	Dan Larson
546	7-05-77	Houston	1B	Bo McLaughlin
547	7-06-77	at San Francisco	1B	Randy Moffitt
548	7-06-77	at San Francisco	1B	Gary Lavelle
549	7-09-77	at Los Angeles	HR	Don Sutton
550	7-10-77	at Los Angeles (1)	1B	Elias Sosa
551	7-10-77	at Los Angeles (2)	HR	Rick Rhoden
552	7-10-77	at Los Angeles (2)	HR	Rick Rhoden
553	7-12-77	San Francisco	1B	Jim Barr
554	7-12-77	San Francisco	1B	Jim Barr
555	7-12-77	San Francisco	1B	Jim Barr
556	7-13-77	San Francisco	1B	Ed Halicki
557	7-13-77	San Francisco	1B	Gary Lavelle
558	7-16-77	Los Angeles	2B	Tommy John
559	7-17-77	Los Angeles	1B	Doug Rau
560	7-17-77	Los Angeles	1B	Doug Rau
561	7-23-77	New York	2B	Jerry Koosman
562	7-24-77	Philadelphia	2B	Jim Kaat
563	7-24-77	Philadelphia	2B	Jim Kaat

Dave was named the Padres' Most Valuable Player in 1978 and 1979. ▶

▼ Dave takes time to discuss the Padres' outlook during spring training, 1975.

NO.	DATE	OPPONENT	HIT	PITCHER
564	7-26-77	Montreal (1)	1B	Jackie Brown
565	7-29-77	at New York	1B	Jerry Koosman
566	7-30-77	at New York	1B	Nino Espinosa
567	7-30-77	at New York	1B	Bob Apodaca
568	7-31-77	at New York	2B	Craig Swan
569	7-31-77	at New York	1B	Craig Swan
570	8-03-77	at Philadelphia	1B	Steve Carlton
571	8-03-77	at Philadelphia	1B	Steve Carlton
572	8-05-77	at Chicago	HR	Pete Broberg
573	8-08-77	at Montreal	1B	Don Stanhouse
574	8-09-77	at Montreal	1B	Fred Holdsworth
575	8-09-77	at Montreal	1B	Bill Atkinson
576	8-10-77	Atlanta (1)	2B	Phil Niekro
577	8-10-77	Atlanta (1)	1B	Phil Niekro
578	8-10-77	Atlanta (1)	2B	Phil Niekro
579	8-10-77	Atlanta (2)	2B	Duane Theiss
580	8-11-77	Atlanta	1B	Preston Hanna
581	8-11-77	Atlanta	2B	Preston Hanna
582	8-12-77	Houston	1B	Tom Dixon
583	8-14-77	Houston	2B	Joe Niekro
584	8-21-77	at St. Louis	1B	Tom Underwood
585	8-21-77	at St. Louis	1B	Clay Carroll
586	8-21-77	at St. Louis	1B	Rawley Eastwick
587	8-22-77	at Pittsburgh	1B	Jim Rooker
588	8-27-77	Pittsburgh	2B	Jerry Reuss
589	8-27-77	Pittsburgh	1B	Jerry Reuss
590	8-28-77	Pittsburgh	1B	Jim Rooker
591	8-31-77	St. Louis	1B	Tom Underwood
592	8-31-77	St. Louis	1B	Butch Metzger
593	9-02-77	Chicago	1B	Mike Krukow
594	9-02-77	Chicago	HR	Dave Giusti
595	9-03-77	Chicago	1B	Rick Reuschel
596	9-03-77	Chicago	1B	Rick Reuschel
597	9-03-77	Chicago	2B	Bruce Sutter
598	9-06-77	Los Angeles	HR	Mike Garman
599	9-07-77	at Houston	2B	J.R. Richard
600	9-07-77	at Houston	1B	J.R. Richard
601	9-09-77	at Atlanta	1B	Preston Hanna
602	9-12-77	at Los Angeles	1B	Mike Garman
603	9-13-77	at Los Angeles	1B	Dennis Lewallyn
604	9-14-77	Atlanta	1B	Preston Hanna
605	9-14-77	Atlanta	HR	Max Leon
606	9-15-77	Atlanta	1B	Steve Hargan
607	9-16-77	Houston	1B	Joaquin Andujar
608	9-20-77	Cincinnati	1B	Tom Seaver
609	9-22-77	Cincinnati	1B	Doug Capilla
610	9-24-77	San Francisco	1B	John Montefusco
611	9-27-77	at Cincinnati	1B	Fred Norman
612	9-27-77	at Cincinnati	2B	Fred Norman
613	9-28-77	at Cincinnati	2B	Paul Moskau
614	10-2-77	at San Francisco	3B	Jim Barr
615	10-2-77	at San Francisco	2B	Jim Barr
616	4-07-78	at San Francisco	1B	John Montefusco
617	4-07-78	at San Francisco	2B	John Montefusco
618	4-07-78	at San Francisco	HR	Gary Lavelle
619	4-08-78	at San Francisco	1B	Jim Barr
620	4-09-78	at San Francisco	3B	Lynn McGlothen
621	4-10-78	at Atlanta	1B	Preston Hanna
622	4-10-78	at Atlanta	HR	Preston Hanna
623	4-11-78	at Atlanta	1B	Phil Niekro
624	4-11-78	at Atlanta	1B	Phil Niekro
625	4-18-78	Houston	2B	Joe Niekro
626	4-19-78	Houston	1B	Joaquin Andujar
627	4-19-78	Houston	HR	Joaquin Andujar
628	4-21-78	Atlanta	1B	Adrian Devine
629	4-21-78	Atlanta	1B	Dave Campbell
630	4-22-78	Atlanta	1B	Tommy Boggs
631	4-22-78	Atlanta	1B	Tommy Boggs
632	4-23-78	Atlanta	1B	Dick Ruthven
633	4-25-78	at Houston	HR	Mark Lemongello
634	4-25-78	at Houston	2B	Mark Lemongello
635	4-28-78	at Philadelphia	1B	Larry Christenson
636	4-28-78	at Philadelphia	HR	Larry Christenson
637	4-30-78	at Philadelphia	1B	Randy Lerch
638	4-30-78	at Philadelphia	1B	Ron Reed
639	5-01-78	at Pittsburgh	HR	Jim Rooker
640	5-06-78	at St. Louis	2B	John Denny
641	5-07-78	at St. Louis	1B	Bob Forsch
642	5-09-78	Chicago	1B	Woodie Fryman
643	5-09-78	Chicago	1B	Bruce Sutter
644	5-10-78	Chicago	1B	Dave A. Roberts
645	5-11-78	Chicago	1B	Bruce Sutter
646	5-12-78	Pittsburgh	1B	Kent Tekulve
647	5-13-78	Pittsburgh	1B	Jerry Reuss
648	5-13-78	Pittsburgh	1B	Bruce Kison

NO.	DATE	OPPONENT	HIT	PITCHER
649	5-15-78	St. Louis	1B	Bob Forsch
650	5-15-78	St. Louis	2B	Dave Hamilton
651	5-21-78	at Cincinnati (1)	1B	Manny Sarmiento
652	5-21-78	at Cincinnati (1)	1B	Dave Tomlin
653	5-21-78	at Cincinnati (1)	1B	Pedro Borbon
654	5-21-78	at Cincinnati (2)	1B	Tom Seaver
655	5-21-78	at Cincinnati (2)	1B	Tom Seaver
656	5-22-78	Los Angeles	1B	Don Sutton
657	5-22-78	Los Angeles	1B	Don Sutton
658	5-23-78	Los Angeles	1B	Tommy John
659	5-24-78	Los Angeles	1B	Charlie Hough
660	5-29-78	at Los Angeles	2B	Tommy John
661	5-30-78	at Los Angeles	1B	Rick Rhoden
662	5-31-78	at Los Angeles	1B	Doug Rau
663	6-02-78	at New York	HR	Nino Espinosa
664	6-03-78	at New York	1B	Pat Zachry
665	6-03-78	at New York	1B	Skip Lockwood
666	6-04-78	at New York	2B	Jerry Koosman
667	6-05-78	at Montreal	1B	Mike Garman
668	6-06-78	at Montreal	1B	Bill Atkinson
669	6-10-78	at Chicago	HR	Dave A. Roberts
670	6-10-78	at Chicago	1B	Dave A. Roberts
671	6-10-78	at Chicago	HR	Donnie Moore
672	6-11-78	at Chicago	1B	Ray Burris
673	6-11-78	at Chicago	1B	Donnie Moore
674	6-12-78	New York	HR	Pat Zachry
675	6-12-78	New York	2B	Pat Zachry
676	6-13-78	New York	1B	Craig Swan
677	6-14-78	Montreal (1)	HR	Wayne Twitchell
678	6-14-78	Montreal (1)	1B	Bill Atkinson
679	6-14-78	Montreal (2)	1B	Woodie Fryman
680	6-14-78	Montreal (2)	1B	Woodie Fryman
681	6-15-78	Montreal	1B	Ross Grimsley
682	6-16-78	Philadelphia	1B	Steve Carlton
683	6-17-78	Philadelphia	2B	Jim Lonborg
684	6-17-78	Philadelphia	2B	Ron Reed
685	6-20-78	Atlanta	1B	Phil Niekro
686	6-23-78	Houston	1B	Tom Dixon
687	6-23-78	Houston	2B	Tom Dixon
688	6-24-78	Houston	HR	Floyd Bannister
689	6-25-78	Houston (1)	1B	J.R. Richard
690	6-25-78	Houston (1)	1B	Rick Williams
691	6-25-78	Houston (2)	1B	Bo McLaughlin
692	6-26-78	San Francisco	HR	Bob Knepper
693	6-26-78	San Francisco	1B	Gary Lavelle
694	6-27-78	San Francisco	1B	Vida Blue
695	6-28-78	San Francisco (2)	HR	Charlie Williams
696	6-30-78	at Houston	1B	J.R. Richard
697	6-30-78	at Houston	1B	J.R. Richard
698	7-01-78	at Houston (1)	1B	Mark Lemongello
699	7-01-78	at Houston (2)	1B	Joe Niekro
700	7-01-78	at Houston (2)	1B	Dick Williams
701	7-01-78	at Houston (2)	1B	Ken Forsch
702	7-03-78	at San Francisco	1B	Jim Barr
703	7-03-78	at San Francisco	1B	Gary Lavelle
704	7-04-78	at San Francisco	HR	John Montefusco
705	7-04-78	at San Francisco	1B	John Montefusco
706	7-05-78	at San Francisco	1B	Ed Halicki
707	7-06-78	at San Francisco	1B	Bob Knepper
708	7-07-78	at Atlanta	2B	Mickey Mahler
709	7-08-78	at Atlanta (1)	1B	Rick Camp
710	7-08-78	at Atlanta (2)	HR	Jamie Easterly
711	7-13-78	at Chicago	2B	Rick Reuschel
712	7-13-78	at Chicago	1B	Donnie Moore
713	7-16-78	at Pittsburgh (1)	1B	Jim Bibby
714	7-16-78	at Pittsburgh (1)	2B	Jim Bibby
715	7-16-78	at Pittsburgh (2)	1B	Grant Jackson
716	7-16-78	at Pittsburgh (2)	2B	Grant Jackson
717	7-17-78	at Pittsburgh	1B	Dave Hamilton
718	7-19-78	at St. Louis	3B	Roy Thomas
719	7-21-78	Chicago	1B	Rick Reuschel
720	7-21-78	Chicago	2B	Rick Reuschel
721	7-23-78	Chicago	1B	Dennis Lamp
722	7-25-78	Pittsburgh	HR	Jim Rooker
723	7-25-78	Pittsburgh	1B	Kent Tekulve
724	7-27-78	Pittsburgh	1B	Jim Bibby
725	7-28-78	St. Louis	1B	John Denny
726	7-29-78	St. Louis	2B	Pete Vuckovich
727	7-29-78	St. Louis	1B	Pete Vuckovich
728	7-30-78	St. Louis	1B	Bob Forsch
729	7-30-78	St. Louis	HR	Bob Forsch
730	7-31-78	Los Angeles	1B	Rick Rhoden
731	8-01-78	Los Angeles	1B	Burt Hooton
732	8-02-78	Los Angeles	1B	Tommy John
733	8-09-78	at Los Angeles	2B	Doug Rau

◀ A versatile Winfield plays first base for the Padres.

There was another incident involving Hall of Fame first baseman Willie McCovey, who joined the Padres in 1974. McCovey says he will never forget the night he stood at the plate in San Diego and watched Winfield end a game by being tagged out attempting to steal home.

"I had no idea he was coming," McCovey says. "It was a rookie mistake. Dave has always been the kind of player who tries to make things happen. I was impressed by his size and his athletic ability. How many guys are drafted to play three different sports (including the Minnesota Vikings of the NFL, Atlanta Hawks of the NBA and Utah Stars of the ABA)?"

Those first weeks and months with Winfield conflicted with McCovey's

teachings that rookies should be seen but not heard.

"It was the first time I noticed that young players were changing," says McCovey. "When I came up, we only spoke when we were spoken to. But Dave and I became very close. He looked up to me. I'm proud that I had some influence on his career. I'm proud of what he did in 1992 to help his team win the World Series."

Winfield left big footprints during his time in San Diego. He led the Padres with 76 RBI and 23 stolen bases in 1975. In 1976, he led the National League in outfield assists (15). A year later, he had the game-winning hit in his first All-Star appearance. In 1979, he became the first Padre ever to be voted to start an All-Star game. That same year, he

▼ A young fan waits for Dave's signature during a Padres autograph session.

GORDY JONES

35

NO.	DATE	OPPONENT	HIT	PITCHER
734	8-10-78	Cincinnati	1B	Dave Tomlin
735	8-12-78	Cincinnati	1B	Tom Seaver
736	8-12-78	Cincinnati	1B	Tom Seaver
737	8-13-78	Cincinnati	1B	Fred Norman
738	8-13-78	Cincinnati	2B	Fred Norman
739	8-15-78	at New York	1B	Craig Swan
740	8-16-78	at New York	1B	Jerry Koosman
741	8-16-79	at New York	2B	Jerry Koosman
742	8-17-78	at New York	2B	Juan Berenguer
743	8-17-78	at New York	HR	Dwight Bernard
744	8-18-78	at Montreal	1B	Steve Rogers
745	8-20-78	at Montreal	1B	Woodie Fryman
746	8-20-78	at Montreal	3B	Hal Dues
747	8-22-78	at Philadelphia	2B	Larry Christenson
748	8-22-78	at Philadelphia	1B	Larry Christenson
749	8-25-78	New York	1B	Craig Swan
750	8-25-78	New York	HR	Craig Swan
751	8-26-78	New York	HR	Jerry Koosman
752	8-27-78	New York	1B	Nino Espinosa
753	8-28-78	Philadelphia	1B	Jim Kaat
754	8-29-78	Philadelphia	1B	Dick Ruthven
755	8-29-78	Philadelphia	1B	Dick Ruthven
756	8-30-78	Philadelphia	3B	Randy Lerch
757	8-31-78	Montreal	1B	Woodie Fryman
758	8-31-78	Montreal	1B	Woodie Fryman
759	9-01-78	Montreal	2B	Ross Grimsley
760	9-01-78	Montreal	2B	Ross Grimsley
761	9-02-78	Montreal	2B	Scott Sanderson
762	9-02-78	Montreal	2B	Scott Sanderson
763	9-04-78	at Atlanta	1B	Larry McWilliams
764	9-04-78	at Atlanta	1B	Larry McWilliams
765	9-06-78	at Atlanta	3B	Mickey Mahler
766	9-07-78	at Cincinnati	1B	Paul Moskau
767	9-08-78	at Cincinnati	1B	Mike LaCoss
768	9-09-78	at Houston	2B	Joe Niekro
769	9-09-78	at Houston	1B	Joe Niekro
770	9-10-78	at Houston	1B	J.R. Richard
771	9-12-78	Atlanta	HR	Mickey Mahler
772	9-12-78	Atlanta	1B	Mickey Mahler
773	9-12-78	Atlanta	1B	Dave Campbell
774	9-13-78	Cincinnati	1B	Mike LaCoss
775	9-13-78	Cincinnati	1B	Manny Sarmiento
776	9-13-78	Cincinnati	1B	Tom Hume
777	9-14-78	Cincinnati	1B	Bill Bonham
778	9-14-78	Cincinnati	1B	Bill Bonham
779	9-14-78	Cincinnati	1B	Manny Sarmiento
780	9-17-78	Houston	1B	Mark Lemongello
781	9-19-78	San Francisco	1B	Ed Halicki
782	9-20-78	San Francisco	1B	Vida Blue
783	9-21-78	San Francisco	1B	John Montefusco
784	9-22-78	at Los Angeles	1B	Doug Rau
785	9-22-78	at Los Angeles	1B	Doug Rau
786	9-22-78	at Los Angeles	HR	Doug Rau
787	9-22-78	at Los Angeles	1B	Rick Sutcliffe
788	9-23-78	at Los Angeles	HR	Burt Hooton
789	9-23-78	at Los Angeles	1B	Terry Forster
790	9-24-78	at Los Angeles	1B	Bob Welch
791	9-24-78	at Los Angeles	1B	Bob Welch
792	9-26-78	at San Francisco	1B	John Montefusco
793	9-29-78	Los Angeles	2B	Burt Hooton
794	10-1-78	Los Angeles	2B	Don Sutton
795	10-1-78	Los Angeles	1B	Don Sutton
796	10-1-78	Los Angeles	2B	Bobby Castillo
797	4-05-79	at Los Angeles	2B	Burt Hooton
798	4-05-79	at Los Angeles	1B	Burt Hooton
799	4-05-79	at Los Angeles	1B	Burt Hooton
800	4-06-79	at Los Angeles	1B	Don Sutton
801	4-08-79	at Los Angeles	1B	Doug Rau
802	4-08-79	at Los Angeles	1B	Rick Sutcliffe
803	4-10-79	at San Francisco	1B	Vida Blue
804	4-10-79	at San Francisco	HR	Vida Blue
805	4-11-79	at San Francisco	2B	John Montefusco
806	4-11-79	at San Francisco	1B	John Montefusco
807	4-11-79	at San Francisco	1B	Tom Griffin
808	4-12-79	at San Francisco	1B	Bob Knepper
809	4-12-79	at San Francisco	HR	Bob Knepper
810	4-13-79	Cincinnati	2B	Bill Bonham
811	4-13-79	Cincinnati	1B	Frank Pastore
812	4-14-79	Cincinnati	2B	Tom Seaver
813	4-15-79	Cincinnati (1)	1B	Dave Tomlin
814	4-17-79	San Francisco	3B	Bob Knepper
815	4-17-79	San Francisco	1B	Bob Knepper
816	4-18-79	San Francisco	3B	Ed Halicki
817	4-18-79	San Francisco	2B	Ed Halicki
818	4-19-79	San Francisco	2B	Vida Blue

NO.	DATE	OPPONENT	HIT	PITCHER
819	4-19-79	San Francisco	1B	Vida Blue
820	4-20-79	at Atlanta	1B	Rick Matula
821	4-20-79	at Atlanta	1B	Rick Matula
822	4-21-79	at Atlanta	2B	Eddie Solomon
823	4-21-79	at Atlanta	1B	Gene Garber
824	4-22-79	at Atlanta	HR	Larry McWilliams
825	4-22-79	at Atlanta	1B	Adrian Devine
826	4-24-79	at Montreal	1B	Ross Grimsley
827	4-25-79	at Montreal	1B	Steve Rogers
828	4-25-79	at Montreal	2B	Elias Sosa
829	4-28-79	at Philadelphia	2B	Steve Carlton
830	4-28-79	at Philadelphia	1B	Doug Bird
831	4-30-79	at New York	3B	Craig Swan
832	4-30-79	at New York	3B	Craig Swan
833	4-30-79	at New York	1B	Craig Swan
834	5-03-79	Montreal	HR	Scott Sanderson
835	5-04-79	Montreal	HR	Ross Grimsley
836	5-05-79	Montreal	HR	Steve Rogers
837	5-05-79	Montreal	1B	Steve Rogers
838	5-05-79	Montreal	HR	Elias Sosa
839	5-07-79	Philadelphia	1B	Steve Carlton
840	5-07-79	Philadelphia	3B	Steve Carlton
841	5-10-79	Philadelphia	2B	Nino Espinosa
842	5-11-79	New York	1B	Kevin Kobel
843	5-12-79	New York	2B	Pete Falcone
844	5-15-79	at Cincinnati	1B	Tom Hume
845	5-15-79	at Cincinnati	1B	Tom Hume
846	5-16-79	at Cincinnati	1B	Bill Bonham
847	5-16-79	at Cincinnati	1B	Pedro Borbon
848	5-19-79	at Houston	2B	J.R. Richard
849	5-20-79	at Houston (2)	1B	Randy Niemann
850	5-20-79	at Houston (2)	1B	Randy Niemann
851	5-22-79	Los Angeles	1B	Doug Rau
852	5-22-79	Los Angeles	HR	Lerrin LaGrow
853	5-22-79	Los Angeles	1B	Bob Welch
854	5-23-79	Los Angeles	2B	Burt Hooton
855	5-25-79	Houston	1B	Rick Williams
856	5-27-79	Houston	1B	J.R. Richard
857	5-28-79	Houston	1B	Joaquin Andujar
858	5-28-79	Houston	1B	Joaquin Andujar
859	5-28-79	Houston	1B	Joaquin Andujar
860	5-29-79	Atlanta (1)	HR	Tony Brizzolara
861	5-29-79	Atlanta (1)	1B	Tony Brizzolara
862	5-29-79	Atlanta (2)	1B	Phil Niekro
863	5-29-79	Atlanta (2)	1B	Phil Niekro
864	5-29-79	Atlanta (2)	1B	Phil Niekro
865	5-30-79	Atlanta	1B	Bo McLaughlin
866	5-30-79	Atlanta	HR	Bo McLaughlin
867	5-31-79	Atlanta	HR	Rick Matula
868	6-01-79	at Pittsburgh	HR	Ed Whitson
869	6-01-79	at Pittsburgh	HR	Kent Tekulve
870	6-02-79	at Pittsburgh	1B	John Candelaria
871	6-05-79	at Chicago	3B	Dennis Lamp
872	6-05-79	at Chicago	2B	Dennis Lamp
873	6-06-79	at Chicago	1B	Rick Reuschel
874	6-07-79	at Chicago	1B	Ken Holtzman
875	6-07-79	at Chicago	HR	Ken Holtzman
876	6-07-79	at Chicago	2B	Lynn McGlothen
877	6-08-79	at St. Louis	1B	Bob Forsch
878	6-08-79	at St. Louis	3B	Bob Forsch
879	6-09-79	at St. Louis	2B	Pete Vuckovich
880	6-10-79	at St. Louis	1B	Silvio Martinez
881	6-12-79	Pittsburgh	HR	John Candelaria
882	6-13-79	Pittsburgh	1B	Bruce Kison
883	6-14-79	Pittsburgh	1B	Jim Rooker
884	6-15-79	Chicago	1B	Rick Reuschel
885	6-17-79	Chicago	1B	Mike Krukow
886	6-19-79	St. Louis	1B	John Fulgham
887	6-22-79	at Houston	3B	Joe Niekro
888	6-24-79	at Houston	1B	Joaquin Andujar
889	6-25-79	at Los Angeles	1B	Rick Sutcliffe
890	6-27-79	Atlanta (1)	2B	Phil Niekro
891	6-27-79	Atlanta (2)	3B	Larry McWilliams
892	6-29-79	Houston	HR	Joaquin Andujar
893	6-30-79	Houston	1B	J.R. Richard
894	7-02-79	Los Angeles	HR	Burt Hooton
895	7-02-79	Los Angeles	1B	Dennis Lewallyn
896	7-04-79	Los Angeles	HR	Don Sutton
897	7-06-79	at New York	1B	Wayne Twitchell
898	7-06-79	at New York	HR	Tom Hausman
899	7-07-79	at New York	1B	Dale Murray
900	7-08-79	at New York (1)	1B	Kevin Kobel
901	7-08-79	at New York (2)	1B	Andy Hassler
902	7-10-79	at Philadelphia	1B	Nino Espinosa
903	7-11-79	at Philadelphia	HR	Randy Lerch

◀ Dave hit safely in his first six professional games, June 19-28, 1973.

▲ Jogging through the Arizona desert at the Padres' spring training camp in 1975.

NO.	DATE	OPPONENT	HIT	PITCHER
904	7-13-79	at Montreal (1)	HR	Ross Grimsley
905	7-13-79	at Montreal (1)	1B	Ross Grimsley
906	7-13-79	at Montreal (1)	1B	Elias Sosa
907	7-13-79	at Montreal (2)	HR	David Palmer
908	7-13-79	at Montreal (2)	1B	David Palmer
909	7-13-79	at Montreal (2)	1B	Stan Bahnsen
910	7-14-79	at Montreal	1B	Bill Lee
911	7-14-79	at Montreal	1B	Bill Lee
912	7-14-79	at Montreal	2B	Dan Schatzeder
913	7-15-79	at Montreal	1B	Scott Sanderson
914	7-15-79	at Montreal	2B	Elias Sosa
915	7-19-79	New York	HR	Kevin Kobel
916	7-20-79	New York	1B	Craig Swan
917	7-22-79	Philadelphia	2B	Nino Espinosa
918	7-23-79	Philadelphia	1B	Dickie Noles
919	7-23-79	Philadelphia	1B	Dickie Noles
920	7-23-79	Philadelphia	HR	Tug McGraw
921	7-23-79	Philadelphia	1B	Ron Reed
922	7-24-79	Montreal	1B	Steve Rogers
923	7-25-79	Montreal	2B	Bill Lee
924	7-26-79	San Francisco	2B	Ed Whitson
925	7-27-79	San Francisco	2B	Vida Blue
926	7-27-79	San Francisco	1B	Vida Blue
927	7-28-79	San Francisco	1B	John Curtis
928	7-29-79	San Francisco	1B	John Montefusco
929	7-29-79	San Francisco	1B	John Montefusco
930	7-29-79	San Francisco	1B	John Montefusco
931	7-31-79	at Atlanta	1B	Phil Niekro
932	7-31-79	at Atlanta	2B	Phil Niekro
933	7-31-79	at Atlanta	1B	Phil Niekro
934	7-31-79	at Atlanta	1B	Bo McLaughlin
935	7-31-79	at Atlanta	HR	Adrian Devine
936	8-02-79	at Atlanta	1B	Tony Brizzolara
937	8-03-79	at Cincinnati	1B	Bill Bonham
938	8-03-79	at Cincinnati	1B	Doug Bair
939	8-05-79	at Cincinnati	1B	Frank Pastore
940	8-07-79	at San Francisco	1B	Vida Blue
941	8-07-79	at San Francisco	1B	Vida Blue
942	8-08-79	at San Francisco	HR	John Curtis
943	8-12-79	Cincinnati (1)	1B	Tom Seaver
944	8-12-79	Cincinnati (2)	1B	Mike LaCoss
945	8-16-79	at Pittsburgh	1B	Bruce Kison
946	8-17-79	at Chicago	HR	Bill Caudill
947	8-20-79	at St. Louis	1B	Silvio Martinez
948	8-21-79	at St. Louis	1B	Mark Littell
949	8-27-79	Chicago	1B	Mike Krukow
950	8-28-79	Chicago	1B	Rick Reuschel
951	8-29-79	Chicago	1B	Lynn McGlothen
952	8-31-79	St. Louis	HR	John Denny
953	9-01-79	St. Louis	1B	Silvio Martinez
954	9-03-79	San Francisco	2B	Ed Whitson
955	9-05-79	at Houston	1B	Joe Sambito
956	9-07-79	at Atlanta	1B	Eddie Solomon
957	9-07-79	at Atlanta	HR	Eddie Solomon
958	9-08-79	at Atlanta	2B	Bo McLaughlin
959	9-11-79	at Los Angeles	1B	Don Sutton
960	9-11-79	at Los Angeles	1B	Don Sutton
961	9-12-79	at Los Angeles	HR	Charlie Hough
962	9-13-79	at Los Angeles	HR	Dave Patterson
963	9-17-79	Houston	1B	Joe Niekro
964	9-18-79	Houston	1B	Rick Williams
965	9-18-79	Houston	2B	Rick Williams
966	9-19-79	Cincinnati	3B	Bill Bonham
967	9-19-79	Cincinnati	1B	Mario Soto
968	9-20-79	Cincinnati	1B	Doug Bair
969	9-21-79	Los Angeles	1B	Gerald Hannahs
970	9-21-79	Los Angeles	HR	Gerald Hannahs
971	9-23-79	Los Angeles	1B	Jerry Reuss
972	9-25-79	at Cincinnati	1B	Fred Norman
973	9-25-79	at Cincinnati	1B	Fred Norman
974	9-25-79	at Cincinnati	1B	Doug Bair
975	9-26-79	at Cincinnati	HR	Tom Seaver
976	9-26-79	at Cincinnati	1B	Tom Seaver
977	9-28-79	at San Francisco	HR	Ed Whitson
978	9-28-79	at San Francisco	1B	Ed Whitson
979	9-29-79	at San Francisco	1B	Bob Knepper
980	9-29-79	at San Francisco	1B	Bob Knepper
981	4-10-80	San Francisco	2B	Bob Knepper
982	4-10-80	San Francisco	1B	Bob Knepper
983	4-12-80	San Francisco	1B	John Montefusco
984	4-12-80	San Francisco	HR	John Montefusco
985	4-16-80	Los Angeles	1B	Don Stanhouse
986	4-17-80	at San Francisco	1B	Vida Blue
987	4-18-80	at San Francisco	HR	Bob Knepper
988	4-19-80	at San Francisco	1B	Ed Whitson

NO.	DATE	OPPONENT	HIT	PITCHER
989	4-20-80	at San Francisco	1B	John Montefusco
990	4-20-80	at San Francisco	1B	John Montefusco
991	4-24-80	at Atlanta	1B	Doyle Alexander
992	4-25-80	at Los Angeles	HR	Rick Sutcliffe
993	4-26-80	at Los Angeles	1B	Joe Beckwith
994	4-27-80	at Los Angeles	HR	Don Sutton
995	5-01-80	Atlanta	1B	Rick Camp
996	5-03-80	at New York	1B	Craig Swan
997	5-04-80	at New York (1)	1B	Jeff Reardon
998	5-04-80	at New York (2)	1B	John Pacella
999	5-04-80	at New York (2)	1B	Ed Glynn
1000	5-04-80	at New York (2)	1B	Neil Allen
1001	5-06-80	at Chicago	2B	Bill Caudill
1002	5-07-80	at Chicago	1B	Mike Krukow
1003	5-07-80	at Chicago	1B	Dick Tidrow
1004	5-07-80	at Chicago	1B	Bruce Sutter
1005	5-08-80	at Chicago	2B	Bruce Sutter
1006	5-09-80	Pittsburgh	1B	Jim Bibby
1007	5-10-80	Pittsburgh	1B	Don A. Robinson
1008	5-11-80	Pittsburgh	1B	John Candelaria
1009	5-14-80	St. Louis	1B	Roy Thomas
1010	5-15-80	St. Louis	2B	Pete Vuckovich
1011	5-16-80	Chicago	3B	Mike Krukow
1012	5-17-80	Chicago	1B	Bruce Sutter
1013	5-18-80	Chicago	2B	Bruce Sutter
1014	5-22-80	at Pittsburgh	HR	Kent Tekulve
1015	5-23-80	at St. Louis	1B	Jim Kaat
1016	5-24-80	at St. Louis	2B	Donnie Moore
1017	5-25-80	at St. Louis	1B	Pete Vuckovich
1018	5-25-80	at St. Louis	1B	Pete Vuckovich
1019	5-25-80	at St. Louis	1B	Don Hood
1020	5-27-80	at Houston	1B	Joe Niekro
1021	5-27-80	at Houston	1B	Joe Niekro
1022	5-29-80	Cincinnati	2B	Frank Pastore
1023	5-30-80	Cincinnati	1B	Charlie Leibrandt
1024	5-30-80	Cincinnati	HR	Charlie Leibrandt
1025	5-31-80	Cincinnati	1B	Paul Moskau
1026	5-31-80	Cincinnati	1B	Tom Hume
1027	6-01-80	Cincinnati	1B	Mario Soto
1028	6-01-80	Cincinnati	2B	Doug Bair
1029	6-03-80	Houston	1B	Vern Ruhle
1030	6-06-80	at Cincinnati	1B	Frank Pastore
1031	6-11-80	at Montreal	1B	Elias Sosa
1032	6-13-80	at Philadelphia	2B	Dick Ruthven
1033	6-14-80	at Philadelphia	1B	Steve Carlton
1034	6-15-80	at Philadelphia	1B	Lerrin LaGrow
1035	6-18-80	Philadelphia	1B	Steve Carlton
1036	6-19-80	Philadelphia	1B	Bob Walk
1037	6-20-80	Montreal	1B	Scott Sanderson
1038	6-20-80	Montreal	1B	Scott Sanderson
1039	6-20-80	Montreal	1B	Woodie Fryman
1040	6-21-80	Montreal	1B	Charlie Lea
1041	6-22-80	Montreal	1B	Steve Rogers
1042	6-22-80	Montreal	2B	Steve Rogers
1043	6-25-80	San Francisco	HR	Allen Ripley
1044	6-25-80	San Francisco	3B	Al Holland
1045	6-26-80	San Francisco	1B	Ed Whitson
1046	6-28-80	Atlanta (1)	2B	Tommy Boggs
1047	6-28-80	Atlanta (1)	1B	Tommy Boggs
1048	6-28-80	Atlanta (2)	1B	Phil Niekro
1049	6-28-80	Atlanta (2)	1B	Phil Niekro
1050	6-29-80	Atlanta	2B	Larry McWilliams
1051	6-29-80	Atlanta	1B	Larry McWilliams
1052	6-30-80	at Los Angeles	1B	Bob Welch
1053	7-01-80	at Los Angeles	HR	Jerry Reuss
1054	7-02-80	at Los Angeles	HR	Dave Goltz
1055	7-02-80	at Los Angeles	1B	Dave Goltz
1056	7-02-80	at Los Angeles	1B	Charlie Hough
1057	7-02-80	at Los Angeles	1B	Rick Sutcliffe
1058	7-02-80	at Los Angeles	1B	Rick Sutcliffe
1059	7-03-80	at Los Angeles	1B	Burt Hooton
1060	7-03-80	at Los Angeles	2B	Burt Hooton
1061	7-04-80	at Atlanta	1B	Larry McWilliams
1062	7-05-80	at Atlanta	1B	Rick Matula
1063	7-05-80	at Atlanta	1B	Rick Matula
1064	7-06-80	at Atlanta	1B	Doyle Alexander
1065	7-06-80	at Atlanta	1B	Doyle Alexander
1066	7-11-80	at San Francisco	1B	Ed Whitson
1067	7-12-80	Los Angeles	3B	Don Sutton
1068	7-13-80	Los Angeles	1B	Bob Welch
1069	7-15-80	at St. Louis	1B	Bob Forsch
1070	7-15-80	at St. Louis	2B	Bob Forsch
1071	7-18-80	at Chicago	1B	Doug Capilla
1072	7-22-80	Pittsburgh	1B	Jim Bibby
1073	7-22-80	Pittsburgh	HR	Enrique Romo

Dave ranks in the Padres' all-time top five in hits, runs, home runs and RBI. ▶

▲ Dave's first professional team, the 1973 Padres.

won his first Gold Glove and had his first 100-RBI season.

Through it all, Winfield felt unfulfilled. The Padres never finished higher than fourth in the NL West during his time in San Diego. Their average annual attendance during that period was only 1,116,491.

"Dave was young and he was impatient. He wanted to play in a larger market and for a contending team," says former Padres president Ballard Smith, who had many difficult contract negotiations over the years with Winfield's agent, Al Frohman.

Smith's suspicions that Frohman wanted Winfield to wind up in New York were confirmed on December 15, 1980, when the veteran left the Padres as a free agent to sign an unprecedented, 10-year, $23 million contract with the Yankees.

"My recollection is that we offered Dave $1 million a year for five years," Smith says. "We never had a chance. It's a tribute to what a great athlete Dave is that he's still playing and having a Hall of Fame career."

Don Zimmer on Winfield
Don Zimmer, Colorado Rockies coach and Winfield's first manager with San Diego.

When I was managing in San Diego, he was the number one draft choice out of Minnesota. (Padres' general manager) Buzzie (Bavasi) signed him and said that he'd work out with us at home—we were only going to be there for three days—then come on the road with us for a week. After we returned home, Winfield was supposed to go to Alexandria in the Texas League. Well, the week goes by and he's hitting balls deep into the seats and catching everything hit his way. I called Buzzie and asked him what the plans for Winfield were and he tells me, "He's going to Alexandria when you get home." I said, "No, I want him to play left field at home on Monday night." He played left field for me on Monday and ended up never spending a day in the minors. David is a great, great player and one of the classiest individuals I've ever managed. I was lucky enough to coach in New York when he played there also. Three years ago people thought he was finished with a bad back. I saw him in spring training in Arizona and told him how nice it was to see him back at it, and he said he was going to play another three or four years. He's a real credit to baseball.

NO.	DATE	OPPONENT	HIT	PITCHER
1074	7-23-80	Pittsburgh	1B	Rick Rhoden
1075	7-24-80	Pittsburgh	HR	Bert Blyleven
1076	7-25-80	St. Louis	2B	Bob Sykes
1077	7-29-80	Chicago	1B	Doug Capilla
1078	7-30-80	Chicago	2B	Lynn McGlothen
1079	7-30-80	Chicago	1B	Bruce Sutter
1080	8-01-80	at Pittsburgh	1B	Jim Bibby
1081	8-03-80	at Pittsburgh (1)	2B	Rick Rhoden
1082	8-03-80	at Pittsburgh (2)	1B	Enrique Romo
1083	8-04-80	at Cincinnati (2)	HR	Joe Price
1084	8-04-80	at Cincinnati (2)	1B	Joe Price
1085	8-06-80	at Cincinnati	HR	Charlie Leibrandt
1086	8-07-80	at Houston	1B	Joe Niekro
1087	8-08-80	at Houston	1B	Vern Ruhle
1088	8-08-80	at Houston	2B	Vern Ruhle
1089	8-10-80	at Houston	1B	Joaquin Andujar
1090	8-10-80	at Houston	1B	Joe Sambito
1091	8-11-80	Cincinnati	1B	Tom Hume
1092	8-14-80	Houston	1B	Nolan Ryan
1093	8-15-80	Houston	1B	Frank LaCorte
1094	8-15-80	Houston	1B	Dave Smith
1095	8-19-80	at Philadelphia	1B	Dick Ruthven
1096	8-20-80	at Philadelphia	1B	Nino Espinosa
1097	8-20-80	at Philadelphia	HR	Nino Espinosa
1098	8-21-80	at Philadelphia	1B	Bob Walk
1099	8-21-80	at Philadelphia	HR	Ron Reed
1100	8-22-80	at Montreal	1B	Fred Norman
1101	8-22-80	at Montreal	HR	Fred Norman
1102	8-24-80	at Montreal	2B	Charlie Lea
1103	8-24-80	at Montreal	1B	Charlie Lea
1104	8-24-80	at Montreal	1B	John D'Acquisto
1105	8-26-80	at New York	1B	Mark Bomback
1106	8-26-80	at New York	HR	Tom Hausman
1107	8-27-80	at New York	HR	Dyar Miller
1108	8-29-80	Philadelphia	2B	Tug McGraw
1109	8-30-80	Philadelphia (1)	3B	Dick Ruthven
1110	8-30-80	Philadelphia (2)	1B	Nino Espinosa
1111	8-30-80	Philadelphia (2)	1B	Nino Espinosa
1112	8-31-80	Philadelphia	1B	Ron Reed
1113	9-01-80	Montreal	2B	Scott Sanderson
1114	9-03-80	Montreal	1B	Fred Norman
1115	9-10-80	San Francisco	HR	Bob Knepper
1116	9-10-80	San Francisco	1B	Greg Minton
1117	9-14-80	at Atlanta	1B	Doyle Alexander
1118	9-18-80	at Los Angeles	1B	Bobby Castillo
1119	9-19-80	Atlanta	3B	Doyle Alexander
1120	9-20-80	Atlanta	1B	Tommy Boggs
1121	9-20-80	Atlanta	1B	Tommy Boggs
1122	9-20-80	Atlanta	1B	Rick Camp
1123	9-23-80	Houston	1B	Randy Niemann
1124	9-23-80	Houston	1B	Bert Roberge
1125	9-24-80	Cincinnati	2B	Tom Hume
1126	9-25-80	Cincinnati	1B	Charlie Leibrandt
1127	9-25-80	Cincinnati	1B	Charlie Leibrandt
1128	9-25-80	Cincinnati	HR	Charlie Leibrandt
1129	9-26-80	Los Angeles	2B	Dave Goltz
1130	9-27-80	Los Angeles	1B	Steve Howe
1131	9-28-80	Los Angeles	2B	Steve Howe
1132	10-3-80	at San Francisco	1B	Allen Ripley
1133	10-4-80	at San Francisco	3B	Ed Whitson
1134	10-4-80	at San Francisco	2B	Mike Rowland

1981•1990

Mixed Memories

BY MOSS KLEIN
NEWARK STAR-LEDGER

To understand the paradox of Dave Winfield's career with the New York Yankees, a consistently successful, yet persistently troublesome stretch that covered 9½ intriguing seasons, consider the events on the night of September 14, 1985.

During that game against the Toronto Blue Jays at Yankee Stadium, a crucial meeting that began with the Yankees trailing Toronto by 2½ games with three weeks remaining, Winfield drove in a first-inning run. That gave him 100 RBI for the season, making him the first Yankee to have four consecutive 100-RBI seasons since Yogi Berra did it from 1953 to 1956.

But in the eighth inning, with the Yankees trailing, 7-2, en route to a 7-4 loss that would drop the club yet another game behind the Blue Jays, George Steinbrenner

Moss Klein is the Assistant Sports Editor for the Newark Star-Ledger. Klein covered Dave Winfield as a member of the New York Yankees from 1981-1990.

Yogi Berra on Winfield
Yogi Berra, Winfield's New York Yankee manager and coach from 1981-85.

Dave Winfield is one of my all-time favorite guys. He's always hustled all the way and kept his body in good shape by taking care of himself. What a good guy. I can't think of another player who hits the ball harder than he does. The way he goes it's a wonder he hasn't killed a pitcher yet. Dave is a great athlete who could've played any sport he wanted, but I'm glad he chose baseball and I'm glad I got the chance to manage and coach a player like him. What more can you say about a guy like that.

◀ Dave becomes a Yankee, December 15, 1980.

strode into the press box, and without being asked a question, said: "Does anyone know where I can find Reggie Jackson? I used to have Mr. October, now I have Winfield, Mr. May."

Winfield's crime that night had been grounding into a double play in the third inning. Sadly, the Winfield-Steinbrenner relationship often overshadowed the performance of the player who was among the best in the team's glorious history. Under different circumstances, Winfield would have remained a Yankee forever, his uniform No. 31 would have joined the club's storied list of retired numbers, a plaque extolling his feats would have ultimately been erected in Yankee Stadium's Monument Park and he would have planned to enter the Hall of Fame — if he ever retires — as a proud Yankee.

"My time with the Yankees could have been so special, so memorable," Winfield says. "I have a lot of great memories of my years there. But we know that those years weren't what they should have been, and we know why."

Winfield, 29 years old during his first Yankee season in 1981, was a dominant force from the start. A remarkable athlete, a well-spoken man, a world traveler and entrepreneur, he seemed to be made for life in the bright lights of the big city. And he was always able to back up his confident words with his deeds.

During his first eight seasons with the Yankees, before missing the 1989 season following back surgery, he drove in 812 runs, most in the majors, hit 203 homers, batted .291 and performed awesome feats

NO.	DATE	OPPONENT	HIT	PITCHER
1135	4-09-81	Texas	1B	Jon Matlack
1136	4-09-81	Texas	1B	Steve Comer
1137	4-11-81	Texas	1B	Danny Darwin
1138	4-12-81	Texas	1B	John Henry Johnson
1139	4-13-81	at Toronto	2B	Jim Clancy
1140	4-15-81	at Toronto	1B	Joey McLaughlin
1141	4-17-81	at Texas	1B	Danny Darwin
1142	4-19-81	at Texas	2B	Jon Matlack
1143	4-20-81	Detroit	1B	Dave Rozema
1144	4-20-81	Detroit	1B	Dave Rozema
1145	4-20-81	Detroit	1B	Dave Tobik
1146	4-22-81	Detroit	1B	Howard Bailey
1147	4-22-81	Detroit	1B	Aurelio Lopez
1148	4-24-81	Toronto	1B	Mark Bomback
1149	4-24-81	Toronto	1B	Mark Bomback
1150	4-25-81	Toronto	2B	Jackson Todd
1151	4-26-81	Toronto	2B	Dave Stieb
1152	4-28-81	at Detroit	2B	Dan Schatzeder
1153	4-29-81	at Detroit	HR	Jack Morris
1154	5-01-81	at Oakland	1B	Rick Langford
1155	5-01-81	at Oakland	1B	Jeff Jones
1156	5-02-81	at Oakland	1B	Matt Keough
1157	5-03-81	at Oakland (1)	1B	Steve McCatty
1158	5-03-81	at Oakland (1)	2B	Steve McCatty
1159	5-03-81	at Oakland (2)	1B	Brian Kingman
1160	5-05-81	at California	2B	Jesse Jefferson
1161	5-05-81	at California	1B	Jesse Jefferson
1162	5-05-81	at California	1B	Don Aase
1163	5-06-81	at California	1B	John D'Acquisto
1164	5-08-81	at Seattle	1B	Bryan Clark
1165	5-08-81	at Seattle	1B	Bryan Clark
1166	5-08-81	at Seattle	1B	Bryan Clark
1167	5-09-81	at Seattle	HR	Brian Allard
1168	5-09-81	at Seattle	1B	Dick Drago
1169	5-10-81	at Seattle	HR	Jerry Don Gleaton
1170	5-12-81	Oakland	2B	Rick Langford
1171	5-13-81	Oakland	2B	Matt Keough
1172	5-14-81	Oakland	1B	Mike Norris
1173	5-16-81	Seattle	1B	Jerry Don Gleaton
1174	5-18-81	Kansas City	1B	Paul Splittorff
1175	5-19-81	Kansas City	1B	Rich Gale
1176	5-20-81	Kansas City	1B	Larry Gura
1177	5-22-81	Cleveland	1B	Bert Blyleven
1178	5-23-81	Cleveland	HR	Rick Waits
1179	5-24-81	Cleveland	1B	John Denny
1180	5-24-81	Cleveland	1B	John Denny
1181	5-26-81	at Baltimore	2B	Scott McGregor
1182	5-27-81	at Baltimore	1B	Mike Flanagan
1183	5-27-81	at Baltimore	1B	Mike Flanagan
1184	5-29-81	at Cleveland	1B	Rick Waits
1185	5-29-81	at Cleveland	1B	Bob Lacey
1186	5-30-81	at Cleveland	1B	Dan Spillner
1187	5-31-81	at Cleveland	1B	Len Barker
1188	6-01-81	at Cleveland	1B	Wayne Garland
1189	6-01-81	at Cleveland	HR	Wayne Garland
1190	6-02-81	Baltimore	2B	Mike Flanagan

NO.	DATE	OPPONENT	HIT	PITCHER
1191	6-02-81	Baltimore	HR	Mike Flanagan
1192	6-03-81	Baltimore	1B	Tippy Martinez
1193	6-04-81	Baltimore	1B	Steve Luebber
1194	6-05-81	Chicago	1B	Britt Burns
1195	6-07-81	Chicago	2B	Ross Baumgarten
1196	6-08-81	at Kansas City	3B	Rich Gale
1197	6-08-81	at Kansas City	1B	Rich Gale
1198	6-09-81	at Kansas City	HR	Juan Berenguer
1199	6-10-81	at Chicago	2B	Britt Burns
1200	6-10-81	at Chicago	1B	LaMarr Hoyt
1201	6-10-81	at Chicago	1B	LaMarr Hoyt
1202	6-11-81	at Chicago	1B	Steve Trout
1203	8-12-81	Texas	2B	Jon Matlack
1204	8-13-81	at Detroit	1B	Dan Petry
1205	8-13-81	at Detroit	1B	George Capuzzello
1206	8-18-81	Chicago	1B	Steve Trout
1207	8-19-81	Chicago	1B	Richard Dotson
1208	8-23-81	Kansas City	1B	Rich Gale
1209	8-23-81	Kansas City	2B	Atlee Hammaker
1210	8-24-81	Minnesota	2B	Brad Havens
1211	8-25-81	Minnesota	2B	Darrell Jackson
1212	8-27-81	at Chicago	1B	Britt Burns
1213	8-27-81	at Chicago	2B	LaMarr Hoyt
1214	8-28-81	at Chicago	1B	Steve Trout
1215	8-28-81	at Chicago	1B	Lynn McGlothen
1216	8-29-81	at Chicago	1B	Kevin Hickey
1217	8-29-81	at Chicago	HR	LaMarr Hoyt
1218	8-30-81	at Chicago	1B	Dennis Lamp
1219	8-31-81	at Minnesota	1B	Al Williams
1220	8-31-81	at Minnesota	1B	Al Williams
1221	8-31-81	at Minnesota	2B	Al Williams
1222	9-01-81	at Minnesota	1B	Pete Redfern
1223	9-01-81	at Minnesota	1B	Jack O'Connor
1224	9-02-81	at Minnesota	1B	Don Cooper
1225	9-03-81	at Kansas City	2B	Mike Jones
1226	9-04-81	at Kansas City	1B	Paul Splittorff
1227	9-06-81	at Kansas City	1B	Atlee Hammaker
1228	9-06-81	at Kansas City	2B	Rich Gale
1229	9-06-81	at Kansas City	1B	Rich Gale
1230	9-07-81	Milwaukee	HR	Randy Lerch
1231	9-09-81	Milwaukee (1)	1B	Pete Vuckovich
1232	9-09-81	Milwaukee (1)	1B	Pete Vuckovich
1233	9-12-81	Boston	2B	Bob Ojeda
1234	9-13-81	Boston	HR	John Tudor
1235	9-13-81	Boston	1B	Chuck Rainey
1236	9-14-81	at Milwaukee	1B	Jerry Augustine
1237	9-16-81	at Milwaukee	2B	Randy Lerch
1238	9-16-81	at Milwaukee	1B	Rollie Fingers
1239	9-18-81	at Boston	HR	Frank Tanana
1240	9-19-81	at Boston	1B	Mike Torrez
1241	9-20-81	at Boston	1B	Bruce Hurst
1242	9-24-81	Baltimore	1B	Jim Palmer
1243	9-25-81	Baltimore	2B	Scott McGregor
1244	9-27-81	Baltimore	1B	Dennis Martinez
1245	10-2-81	at Baltimore	HR	Sammy Stewart
1246	10-2-81	at Baltimore	HR	Jeff Schneider
1247	10-2-81	at Baltimore	1B	Mike Boddicker
1248	10-4-81	at Baltimore	2B	Mike Flanagan
1249	4-11-82	Chicago (1)	1B	Jerry Koosman
1250	4-11-82	Chicago (1)	HR	Jerry Koosman
1251	4-11-82	Chicago (2)	1B	Britt Burns
1252	4-12-82	at Texas	HR	Jon Matlack
1253	4-13-82	at Texas	1B	Rick Honeycutt
1254	4-13-82	at Texas	2B	Rick Honeycutt
1255	4-16-82	at Detroit	1B	Pat Underwood
1256	4-16-82	at Detroit	2B	Dave Tobik
1257	4-16-82	at Detroit	2B	Dave Tobik
1258	4-20-82	at Chicago	1B	Dennis Lamp
1259	4-21-82	at Chicago	1B	Richard Dotson
1260	4-22-82	Detroit	1B	Jack Morris
1261	4-24-82	Detroit	1B	Larry Pashnick
1262	4-24-82	Detroit	1B	Larry Pashnick
1263	4-25-82	Detroit	1B	Kevin Saucier
1264	4-28-82	California	2B	Ken Forsch
1265	4-30-82	Seattle	1B	Gaylord Perry
1266	4-30-82	Seattle	2B	Gaylord Perry
1267	5-02-82	Seattle	1B	Floyd Bannister
1268	5-02-82	Seattle	1B	Mike T. Stanton
1269	5-04-82	Oakland	1B	Tom Underwood
1270	5-04-82	Oakland	2B	Jeff Jones
1271	5-04-82	Oakland	HR	Bob Owchinko
1272	5-06-82	at Seattle	1B	Gaylord Perry
1273	5-08-82	at Seattle	1B	Jim Beattie
1274	5-08-82	at Seattle	1B	Mike T. Stanton
1275	5-09-82	at Seattle	2B	Gene Nelson

▼ Opponents are forced to hit the ball farther than normal to get it over Dave's 6'6" frame.

New York Yankees

New York Yankees

▲ 1,300 of Dave's 3,000 hits came in a Yankee uniform.

New York Yankees

▲ Patrolling Yankee Stadium's left field in 1981.

NO.	DATE	OPPONENT	HIT	PITCHER
1276	5-09-82	at Seattle	2B	Gene Nelson
1277	5-10-82	at California	HR	Geoff Zahn
1278	5-10-82	at California	2B	Geoff Zahn
1279	5-12-82	at California	1B	Mike Witt
1280	5-13-82	at Oakland	1B	Tom Underwood
1281	5-14-82	at Oakland	1B	Matt Keough
1282	5-14-82	at Oakland	HR	Dave Beard
1283	5-15-82	at Oakland	1B	Rick Langford
1284	5-16-82	at Oakland	3B	Steve McCatty
1285	5-18-82	at Kansas City	1B	Dave Frost
1286	5-18-82	at Kansas City	1B	Dave Frost
1287	6-09-82	at Boston	HR	Bruce Hurst
1288	6-09-82	at Boston	1B	Bruce Hurst
1289	6-10-82	at Boston	HR	John Tudor
1290	6-11-82	at Baltimore	2B	Dennis Martinez
1291	6-11-82	at Baltimore	3B	Dennis Martinez
1292	6-14-82	Boston	1B	Luis Aponte
1293	6-15-82	Boston	2B	Bruce Hurst
1294	6-16-82	Boston	1B	John Tudor
1295	6-18-82	Baltimore	HR	Jim Palmer
1296	6-18-82	Baltimore	1B	Jim Palmer
1297	6-19-82	Baltimore	1B	Scott McGregor
1298	6-19-82	Baltimore	1B	Scott McGregor
1299	6-19-82	Baltimore	1B	Scott McGregor
1300	6-20-82	Baltimore	1B	Mike Flanagan
1301	6-24-82	Cleveland	1B	Rick Sutcliffe
1302	6-25-82	Cleveland	1B	Len Barker
1303	6-25-82	Cleveland	2B	Bud Anderson
1304	6-25-82	Cleveland	1B	Bud Anderson
1305	6-25-82	Cleveland	1B	Bud Anderson
1306	6-29-82	Milwaukee	HR	Mike Caldwell
1307	6-29-82	Milwaukee	1B	Mike Caldwell
1308	6-30-82	Milwaukee	1B	Randy Lerch
1309	7-02-82	at Cleveland	HR	Rick Waits
1310	7-02-82	at Cleveland	1B	Rick Waits
1311	7-02-82	at Cleveland	HR	Ed Whitson
1312	7-03-82	at Cleveland	1B	Lary Sorensen
1313	7-03-82	at Cleveland	1B	Dan Spillner
1314	7-03-82	at Cleveland	HR	Dan Spillner
1315	7-04-82	at Cleveland	2B	John Denny
1316	7-05-82	at Seattle	HR	Jim Beattie
1317	7-05-82	at Seattle	1B	Mike T. Stanton
1318	7-06-82	at Seattle	HR	Gaylord Perry
1319	7-06-82	at Seattle	1B	Bryan Clark
1320	7-06-82	at Seattle	1B	Mike T. Stanton
1321	7-07-82	at Oakland	HR	Rick Langford
1322	7-07-82	at Oakland	1B	Rick Langford
1323	7-10-82	at California	1B	Ken Forsch
1324	7-15-82	Oakland	1B	Dave Beard
1325	7-18-82	Oakland	3B	Brian Kingman
1326	7-18-82	Oakland	1B	Tom Underwood
1327	7-19-82	Seattle	HR	Gene Nelson
1328	7-19-82	Seattle	1B	Bryan Clark
1329	7-19-82	Seattle	3B	Bryan Clark
1330	7-21-82	Seattle	HR	Floyd Bannister
1331	7-22-82	Texas	2B	John Butcher
1332	7-22-82	Texas	2B	John Butcher
1333	7-23-82	California	3B	Mike Witt
1334	7-24-82	California	1B	Andy Hassler
1335	7-25-82	California	1B	Dave Goltz
1336	7-25-82	California	1B	Mickey Mahler
1337	7-27-82	Detroit	1B	Jack Morris
1338	7-28-82	Detroit	1B	Larry Pashnick
1339	7-28-82	Detroit	1B	Larry Pashnick
1340	7-30-82	at Texas	3B	Doc Medich
1341	7-31-82	at Texas	1B	Danny Darwin
1342	8-01-82	at Texas	1B	Rick Honeycutt
1343	8-03-82	Chicago (2)	2B	Richard Dotson
1344	8-03-82	Chicago (2)	1B	Richard Dotson
1345	8-04-82	Chicago (1)	1B	LaMarr Hoyt
1346	8-04-82	Chicago (1)	1B	Kevin Hickey
1347	8-06-82	Texas	1B	Rick Honeycutt
1348	8-06-82	Texas	HR	Rick Honeycutt
1349	8-07-82	Texas	1B	Frank Tanana
1350	8-07-82	Texas	1B	Steve Comer
1351	8-08-82	Texas (1)	1B	John Butcher
1352	8-08-82	Texas (2)	1B	Jon Matlack
1353	8-08-82	Texas (2)	1B	Jon Matlack
1354	8-09-82	at Detroit	HR	Dan Petry
1355	8-11-82	at Detroit	1B	Jack Morris
1356	8-16-82	Kansas City (2)	HR	Bud Black
1357	8-16-82	Kansas City (2)	3B	Mike Armstrong
1358	8-17-82	Kansas City	HR	Paul Splittorff
1359	8-17-82	Kansas City	HR	Paul Splittorff
1360	8-18-82	Kansas City	1B	Dave Frost

NO.	DATE	OPPONENT	HIT	PITCHER
1361	8-20-82	Toronto	1B	Dave Stieb
1362	8-20-82	Toronto	HR	Dave Stieb
1363	8-23-82	Toronto	2B	Luis Leal
1364	8-29-82	at Toronto	HR	Jim Clancy
1365	8-29-82	at Toronto	HR	Jim Clancy
1366	8-30-82	at Minnesota	HR	Frank Viola
1367	8-31-82	at Minnesota	1B	Brad Havens
1368	9-01-82	at Minnesota	1B	Al Williams
1369	9-01-82	at Minnesota	3B	Al Williams
1370	9-04-82	at Kansas City	HR	Larry Gura
1371	9-05-82	at Kansas City	2B	Dennis Leonard
1372	9-05-82	at Kansas City	HR	Dennis Leonard
1373	9-05-82	at Kansas City	1B	Don Hood
1374	9-05-82	at Kansas City	HR	Mike Armstrong
1375	9-07-82	Baltimore	1B	Mike Flanagan
1376	9-07-82	Baltimore	1B	Mike Flanagan
1377	9-08-82	Baltimore	HR	Ross Grimsley
1378	9-09-82	Milwaukee	1B	Pete Vuckovich
1379	9-09-82	Milwaukee	HR	Pete Vuckovich
1380	9-10-82	Milwaukee	1B	Mike Caldwell
1381	9-11-82	Milwaukee	1B	Doc Medich
1382	9-11-82	Milwaukee	HR	Jerry Augustine
1383	9-11-82	Milwaukee	1B	Jamie Easterly
1384	9-12-82	Milwaukee	1B	Don Sutton
1385	9-13-82	at Baltimore	HR	Dennis Martinez
1386	9-15-82	at Baltimore	HR	Mike Flanagan
1387	9-16-82	at Baltimore	HR	Jim Palmer
1388	9-16-82	at Baltimore	1B	Jim Palmer
1389	9-18-82	at Milwaukee	HR	Bob McClure
1390	9-21-82	Cleveland (1)	1B	Len Barker
1391	9-25-82	at Boston	2B	Dennis Eckersley
1392	9-26-82	at Boston	2B	Mike Torrez
1393	9-26-82	at Boston	1B	Bob Stanley
1394	9-27-82	at Boston	2B	Tom Burgmeier
1395	9-27-82	at Boston	1B	Oil Can Boyd
1396	9-27-82	at Boston	2B	Mike Brown
1397	9-28-82	at Cleveland	HR	Rick Sutcliffe
1398	9-28-82	at Cleveland	2B	Jerry Reed
1399	9-29-82	at Cleveland	2B	Lary Sorensen
1400	4-05-83	at Seattle	1B	Gaylord Perry
1401	4-05-83	at Seattle	HR	Gaylord Perry
1402	4-06-83	at Seattle	HR	Matt Young
1403	4-07-83	at Seattle	HR	Bryan Clark
1404	4-09-83	at Toronto	1B	Jim Gott
1405	4-10-83	at Toronto	1B	Dave Stieb
1406	4-12-83	Detroit	1B	Dan Petry
1407	4-14-83	Detroit	1B	Jack Morris
1408	4-15-83	Toronto	1B	Dave Stieb
1409	4-17-83	Toronto	HR	Jim Clancy
1410	4-20-83	at Chicago	1B	LaMarr Hoyt
1411	4-22-83	Minnesota	1B	Brad Havens
1412	4-23-83	Minnesota	1B	Jack O'Connor
1413	4-23-83	Minnesota	1B	Jack O'Connor
1414	4-25-83	Minnesota	2B	Frank Viola
1415	4-25-83	Minnesota	3B	Frank Viola
1416	4-26-83	Kansas City	3B	Larry Gura
1417	4-29-83	at Texas	1B	Rick Honeycutt
1418	4-29-83	at Texas	3B	Jon Matlack
1419	5-01-83	at Texas	2B	Mike Smithson
1420	5-01-83	at Texas	1B	Odell Jones
1421	5-04-83	at Kansas City	1B	Bill Castro
1422	5-04-83	at Kansas City	HR	Don Hood
1423	5-06-83	at Minnesota	1B	Jack O'Connor
1424	5-06-83	at Minnesota	1B	Ron Davis
1425	5-07-83	at Minnesota	HR	Frank Viola
1426	5-08-83	at Minnesota	HR	Bobby Castillo
1427	5-10-83	Texas	1B	Danny Darwin
1428	5-11-83	Texas	1B	Rick Honeycutt
1429	5-14-83	Chicago	3B	Britt Burns
1430	5-14-83	Chicago	1B	Dennis Lamp
1431	5-15-83	Chicago	2B	Floyd Bannister
1432	5-15-83	Chicago	2B	Floyd Bannister
1433	5-16-83	at Detroit	1B	Jerry Ujdur
1434	5-17-83	at Detroit	HR	Jack Morris
1435	5-17-83	at Detroit	HR	Jack Morris
1436	5-17-83	at Detroit	1B	Aurelio Lopez
1437	5-17-83	at Detroit	1B	Aurelio Lopez
1438	5-21-83	at Oakland	1B	Mike Norris
1439	5-22-83	at Oakland	2B	Chris Codiroli
1440	5-22-83	at Oakland	1B	Chris Codiroli
1441	5-23-83	at California	1B	Geoff Zahn
1442	5-25-83	at California	1B	Tommy John
1443	5-25-83	at California	1B	Tommy John
1444	5-30-83	Oakland	3B	Steve McCatty
1445	5-31-83	California	2B	Bill Travers

▲ Hitting the dirt against the Angels.

V. J. LOVERO

in the outfield, winning five Rawlings Gold Glove Awards. He made the American League All-Star team every year, became the first Yankee since Joe DiMaggio to drive in 100-plus runs in five consecutive seasons, and the first since the Yankee Clipper to have two consecutive seasons with 100 or more RBI and runs scored.

But as teammates and opponents often pointed out, Winfield's value was hardly limited to numbers.

"The way he plays the game makes him special," said Tigers' manager Sparky Anderson, who had been managing in the National League with Cincinnati when Winfield arrived with the Padres in 1973. "His talent is obvious, that's a gift. But a lot of players have talent. Winfield always plays

Rickey Henderson on Winfield
Rickey Henderson, Toronto Blue Jays outfielder and Winfield's New York Yankee teammate from 1985-89.

Dave Winfield taught me a great deal about the game of baseball both on and off the field. Everyone knows that Dave has been a great player on the field but I don't think he gets enough credit for what he has done off it. The Dave Winfield Foundation is a great example for all of us who play major league baseball of what we can do off the field.

Dave warms up prior to one of his final games as a Yankee in 1990. ▶

JOHN CORDES

NO.	DATE	OPPONENT	HIT	PITCHER
1446	6-02-83	California	HR	Geoff Zahn
1447	6-05-83	Seattle	HR	Gene Nelson
1448	6-07-83	Cleveland	1B	Bert Blyleven
1449	6-08-83	Cleveland	HR	Rick Sutcliffe
1450	6-08-83	Cleveland	2B	Dan Spillner
1451	6-10-83	at Milwaukee	1B	Moose Haas
1452	6-14-83	at Cleveland	1B	Lary Sorensen
1453	6-14-83	at Cleveland	1B	Neal Heaton
1454	6-14-83	at Cleveland	1B	Dan Spillner
1455	6-17-83	Milwaukee	2B	Mike Caldwell
1456	6-17-83	Milwaukee	1B	Tom Tellmann
1457	6-18-83	Milwaukee	1B	Don Sutton
1458	6-18-83	Milwaukee	1B	Don Sutton
1459	6-19-83	Milwaukee	1B	Rick Waits
1460	6-21-83	at Baltimore	1B	Storm Davis
1461	6-24-83	at Boston	1B	John Tudor
1462	6-25-83	at Boston	1B	Dennis Eckersley
1463	6-26-83	at Boston	1B	Bruce Hurst
1464	6-30-83	Baltimore	1B	Dennis Martinez
1465	6-30-83	Baltimore	1B	Tippy Martinez
1466	7-01-83	Boston	2B	Dennis Eckersley
1467	7-02-83	Boston	HR	Bruce Hurst
1468	7-04-83	Boston	1B	John Tudor
1469	7-08-83	at Kansas City	1B	Larry Gura
1470	7-08-83	at Kansas City	1B	Larry Gura
1471	7-08-83	at Kansas City	1B	Larry Gura
1472	7-09-83	at Kansas City	1B	Bud Black
1473	7-10-83	at Kansas City	1B	Paul Splittorff
1474	7-12-83	at Minnesota	1B	Frank Viola
1475	7-12-83	at Minnesota	1B	Rick Lysander
1476	7-13-83	at Minnesota	1B	Ken Schrom
1477	7-13-83	at Minnesota	1B	Ken Schrom
1478	7-14-83	Texas	1B	Charlie Hough
1479	7-15-83	Texas	HR	Rick Honeycutt
1480	7-15-83	Texas	1B	Rick Honeycutt
1481	7-17-83	Texas	1B	Frank Tanana
1482	7-17-83	Texas	2B	Frank Tanana
1483	7-18-83	Minnesota	1B	Al Williams
1484	7-18-83	Minnesota	3B	Al Williams
1485	7-19-83	Minnesota	3B	Len Whitehouse
1486	7-22-83	Kansas City (1)	HR	Gaylord Perry
1487	7-24-83	Kansas City	HR	Bud Black
1488	7-24-83	Kansas City	1B	Bud Black
1489	7-24-83	Kansas City	1B	Mike Armstrong
1490	7-25-83	at Texas	1B	Mike Smithson
1491	7-25-83	at Texas	3B	Odell Jones
1492	7-26-83	at Texas	2B	Frank Tanana
1493	7-27-83	at Texas	1B	Charlie Hough
1494	7-29-83	at Chicago	1B	Jerry Koosman
1495	7-29-83	at Chicago	HR	Jerry Koosman
1496	7-31-83	at Chicago	1B	Britt Burns
1497	8-01-83	at Chicago	HR	Floyd Bannister
1498	8-02-83	at Toronto (1)	1B	Joey McLaughlin
1499	8-02-83	at Toronto (2)	HR	Matt Williams
1500	8-02-83	at Toronto (2)	1B	Roy Lee Jackson
1501	8-04-83	at Toronto	1B	Dave Stieb
1502	8-04-83	at Toronto	2B	Dave Stieb
1503	8-05-83	Detroit	2B	John Martin
1504	8-05-83	Detroit	HR	Larry Pashnick
1505	8-06-83	Detroit	HR	Doug Bair
1506	8-06-83	Detroit	1B	Dave Gumpert
1507	8-06-83	Toronto (1)	2B	Jim Clancy
1508	8-08-83	Toronto (1)	1B	Jim Clancy
1509	8-08-83	Toronto (1)	1B	Jim Clancy
1510	8-08-83	Toronto (2)	HR	Roy Lee Jackson
1511	8-10-83	Toronto	1B	Jim Clancy
1512	8-10-83	Toronto	2B	Roy Lee Jackson
1513	8-11-83	at Detroit	1B	Howard Bailey
1514	8-11-83	at Detroit	HR	Howard Bailey
1515	8-12-83	at Detroit	HR	Dan Petry
1516	8-12-83	at Detroit	HR	Dan Petry
1517	8-12-83	at Detroit	2B	Dan Petry
1518	8-13-83	at Detroit	2B	Jack Morris
1519	8-14-83	at Detroit	2B	Juan Berenguer
1520	8-16-83	Chicago	2B	Floyd Bannister
1521	8-16-83	Chicago	1B	Salome Barojas
1522	8-20-83	California	1B	Tommy John
1523	8-20-83	California	1B	Tommy John
1524	8-22-83	Oakland	1B	Gorman Heimueller
1525	8-24-83	Seattle	1B	Bryan Clark
1526	8-26-83	at California	2B	Geoff Zahn
1527	8-27-83	at California	1B	Rick Steirer
1528	8-28-83	at California	1B	Ken Forsch
1529	8-28-83	at California	1B	Ken Forsch
1530	8-30-83	at Oakland	1B	Dave Beard

NO.	DATE	OPPONENT	HIT	PITCHER
1531	8-31-83	at Oakland	1B	Mark Smith
1532	8-31-83	at Oakland	1B	Mark Smith
1533	9-02-83	at Seattle	HR	Karl Best
1534	9-03-83	at Seattle	1B	Mike Moore
1535	9-03-83	at Seattle	1B	Mike Moore
1536	9-03-83	at Seattle	2B	Mike Moore
1537	9-03-83	at Seattle	1B	Ed VandeBerg
1538	9-07-83	at Milwaukee	2B	Jerry Augustine
1539	9-08-83	at Milwaukee	1B	Bob L. Gibson
1540	9-09-83	Baltimore	2B	Scott McGregor
1541	9-10-83	Baltimore (1)	1B	Sammy Stewart
1542	9-10-83	Baltimore (2)	1B	Mike Boddicker
1543	9-10-83	Baltimore (2)	1B	Tippy Martinez
1544	9-14-83	Milwaukee	1B	Don Sutton
1545	9-14-83	Milwaukee	1B	Don Sutton
1546	9-14-83	Milwaukee	1B	Rick Waits
1547	9-17-83	at Cleveland	HR	Neal Heaton
1548	9-17-83	at Cleveland	HR	Neal Heaton
1549	9-17-83	at Cleveland	1B	Neal Heaton
1550	9-18-83	at Cleveland (1)	1B	Lary Sorensen
1551	9-18-83	at Cleveland (1)	1B	Lary Sorensen
1552	9-18-83	at Cleveland (1)	1B	Mike Jeffcoat
1553	9-18-83	at Cleveland (1)	HR	Bud Anderson
1554	9-18-83	at Cleveland (2)	1B	Rich Barnes
1555	9-18-83	at Cleveland (2)	HR	Tom Brennan
1556	9-18-83	at Cleveland (2)	1B	Dan Spillner
1557	9-19-83	at Boston	1B	John Tudor
1558	9-21-83	at Boston	1B	Bob Ojeda
1559	9-21-83	at Boston	1B	Bob Ojeda
1560	9-21-83	at Boston	2B	Bob Ojeda
1561	9-24-83	Cleveland	2B	Rick Sutcliffe
1562	9-24-83	Cleveland	HR	Rick Sutcliffe
1563	9-24-83	Cleveland	1B	Mike Jeffcoat
1564	9-27-83	Boston	2B	Mark Clear
1565	9-28-83	Boston	1B	Bob Ojeda
1566	9-29-83	Boston	HR	John Tudor
1567	9-30-83	Baltimore (1)	1B	Storm Davis
1568	10-1-83	Baltimore	1B	Scott McGregor
1569	4-03-84	at Kansas City	HR	Bud Black
1570	4-04-84	at Kansas City	2B	Paul Splittorff
1571	4-05-84	at Kansas City	1B	Larry Gura
1572	4-06-84	at Texas	1B	Frank Tanana
1573	4-06-84	at Texas	HR	Frank Tanana
1574	4-06-84	at Texas	1B	Tom Henke
1575	4-06-84	at Texas	1B	Dave Tobik
1576	4-07-84	at Texas	1B	Danny Darwin
1577	4-07-84	at Texas	1B	Danny Darwin
1578	4-10-84	Minnesota	1B	Larry Pashnick
1579	4-15-84	Chicago	1B	LaMarr Hoyt
1580	5-01-84	at Chicago	1B	Bob Fallon
1581	5-01-84	at Chicago	1B	Ron Reed
1582	5-06-84	at Milwaukee	1B	Mike Caldwell
1583	5-06-84	at Milwaukee	2B	Pete Ladd
1584	5-09-84	Cleveland	2B	Rick Sutcliffe
1585	5-09-84	Cleveland	HR	Rick Sutcliffe
1586	5-09-84	Cleveland	1B	Dan Spillner
1587	5-09-84	Cleveland	2B	Dan Spillner
1588	5-11-84	Seattle	HR	Matt Young
1589	5-13-84	Seattle	1B	Mark Langston
1590	5-13-84	Seattle	1B	Mark Langston
1591	5-13-84	Seattle	1B	Bob Stoddard
1592	5-15-84	Oakland	1B	Ray Burris
1593	5-15-84	Oakland	3B	Ray Burris
1594	5-15-84	Oakland	1B	Tim Conroy
1595	5-15-84	Oakland	2B	Chris Codiroli
1596	5-16-84	Oakland	1B	Keith Atherton
1597	5-16-84	Oakland	HR	Bill Caudill
1598	5-19-84	California	1B	Geoff Zahn
1599	5-22-84	at Seattle	1B	Matt Young
1600	5-24-84	at Seattle	2B	Mike T. Stanton
1601	5-25-84	at Oakland	2B	Steve McCatty
1602	5-25-84	at Oakland	1B	Steve McCatty
1603	5-26-84	at Oakland	1B	Lary Sorensen
1604	5-26-84	at Oakland	2B	Lary Sorensen
1605	5-27-84	at Oakland	1B	Ray Burris
1606	5-28-84	at California	1B	Doug Corbett
1607	5-29-84	at California	1B	Frank LaCorte
1608	5-29-84	at California	HR	Craig Swan
1609	5-29-84	at California	1B	Curt Kaufman
1610	5-30-84	at California	1B	Ron Romanick
1611	5-30-84	at California	2B	Jim Slaton
1612	6-01-84	at Toronto	1B	Doyle Alexander
1613	6-02-84	at Toronto	1B	Luis Leal
1614	6-02-84	at Toronto	1B	Jim Gott
1615	6-03-84	at Toronto	1B	Jim Clancy

▲ Dave bunting toward 3,000.

▲ Dave with Hall of Famer Reggie Jackson in December 1980.

Lou Piniella on Winfield
Lou Piniella, Dave's New York Yankee team-mate from 1981-84 and manager from 1986-88.

Dave Winfield is a class gentleman, an excellent athlete, a tremendous baseball player and future Hall of Famer. I really enjoyed getting to know him on a personal basis as a teammate. He's one of the better people that I've ever met in this game. What people don't realize about Dave is how hard he plays on the field and how that affects young kids in the clubhouse. He's a complete person. When I managed him in New York, quite frankly, I wished I'd had 25 individuals in the clubhouse just like him.

Congratulations, Dave, it's been a long road, big fella. You've done a hell of a job and keep doing it as long as you enjoy it. I'd like to be there in Cooperstown when you get in.

hard, he always hustles, he knows how to use his talent. I've always wished I could have had him on my team for a season."

Billy Martin, who was around for three of his five managerial stints with the Yankees during the Winfield years, often tried to persuade Steinbrenner to curtail the controversies because Martin had such respect for Winfield — and such admiration for him as a player.

"There are only a handful of guys who come along each generation who are capable of doing what Winfield can do," Martin once said. "He can beat you in so many ways — with a homer, with a key hit, with his base running, with his speed, with his glove, with his arm. It's a whole lot more fun managing the team he plays for instead of the team he's playing against."

NO.	DATE	OPPONENT	HIT	PITCHER
1616	6-03-84	at Toronto	1B	Jim Acker
1617	6-03-84	at Toronto	1B	Jim Acker
1618	6-03-84	at Toronto	1B	Bryan Clark
1619	6-03-84	at Toronto	1B	Bryan Clark
1620	6-04-84	Boston	3B	Steve Crawford
1621	6-05-84	Boston	1B	Al Nipper
1622	6-05-84	Boston	1B	John Henry Johnson
1623	6-05-84	Boston	1B	Mark Clear
1624	6-05-84	Boston	2B	Mark Clear
1625	6-05-84	Boston	1B	Bob Stanley
1626	6-06-84	Boston	2B	Bruce Hurst
1627	6-08-84	Toronto	1B	Jim Acker
1628	6-09-84	Toronto	1B	Dave Stieb
1629	6-09-84	Toronto	1B	Dave Stieb
1630	6-09-84	Toronto	1B	Dave Stieb
1631	6-10-84	Toronto	1B	Doyle Alexander
1632	6-10-84	Toronto	2B	Doyle Alexander
1633	6-12-84	at Boston	1B	Roger Clemens
1634	6-12-84	at Boston	1B	Steve Crawford
1635	6-13-84	at Boston	2B	Oil Can Boyd
1636	6-13-84	at Boston	HR	Oil Can Boyd
1637	6-13-84	at Boston	2B	Oil Can Boyd
1638	6-14-84	at Boston	1B	Bob Ojeda
1639	6-14-84	at Boston	1B	Bob Stanley
1640	6-16-84	Baltimore	1B	Bill Swaggerty
1641	6-16-84	Baltimore	1B	Sammy Stewart
1642	6-18-84	at Detroit	1B	Milt Wilcox
1643	6-18-84	at Detroit	1B	Willie Hernandez
1644	6-19-84	at Detroit	2B	Carl Willis
1645	6-19-84	at Detroit	1B	Carl Willis
1646	6-19-84	at Detroit	1B	Carl Willis
1647	6-20-84	at Detroit	2B	Dan Petry
1648	6-20-84	at Detroit	HR	Aurelio Lopez
1649	6-20-84	at Detroit	1B	Willie Hernandez
1650	6-21-84	at Baltimore	1B	Scott McGregor
1651	6-21-84	at Baltimore	1B	Scott McGregor
1652	6-21-84	at Baltimore	2B	Sammy Stewart
1653	6-22-84	at Baltimore	1B	Mike Flanagan
1654	6-23-84	at Baltimore	2B	Dennis Martinez
1655	6-23-84	at Baltimore	1B	Dennis Martinez
1656	6-25-84	Detroit	1B	Dan Petry
1657	6-25-84	Detroit	1B	Dan Petry
1658	6-25-84	Detroit	1B	Dan Petry
1659	6-25-84	Detroit	2B	Doug Bair
1660	6-25-84	Detroit	1B	Willie Hernandez
1661	7-01-84	at Kansas City	1B	Charlie Leibrandt
1662	7-01-84	at Kansas City	1B	Dan Quisenberry
1663	7-02-84	at Texas	1B	Danny Darwin
1664	7-02-84	at Texas	HR	Danny Darwin
1665	7-03-84	at Texas	1B	Frank Tanana
1666	7-03-84	at Texas	1B	Odell Jones
1667	7-05-84	at Minnesota	1B	Ken Schrom
1668	7-05-84	at Minnesota	1B	Ken Schrom
1669	7-05-84	at Minnesota	2B	Ken Schrom
1670	7-07-84	at Minnesota	2B	Pete Filson
1671	7-12-84	Kansas City	1B	Larry Gura
1672	7-12-84	Kansas City	1B	Larry Gura
1673	7-13-84	Kansas City (2)	1B	Bret Saberhagen
1674	7-14-84	Kansas City	1B	Mark Huismann
1675	7-16-84	Texas	HR	Dickie Noles
1676	7-18-84	Texas	1B	Mike Mason
1677	7-20-84	Minnesota	1B	Ken Schrom
1678	7-21-84	Minnesota	1B	Mike Smithson
1679	7-21-84	Minnesota	1B	Mike Smithson
1680	7-21-84	Minnesota	1B	Mike Smithson
1681	7-22-84	Minnesota	HR	Frank Viola
1682	7-22-84	Minnesota	1B	Frank Viola
1683	7-27-84	at Chicago	2B	LaMarr Hoyt
1684	7-27-84	at Chicago	2B	Jerry Don Gleaton
1685	7-28-84	at Chicago	2B	Gene Nelson
1686	7-29-84	at Chicago	1B	Floyd Bannister
1687	7-29-84	at Chicago	1B	Floyd Bannister
1688	7-30-84	Milwaukee	1B	Mike Caldwell
1689	8-01-84	Milwaukee	1B	Jaime Cocanower
1690	8-01-84	Milwaukee	1B	Jaime Cocanower
1691	8-01-84	Milwaukee	1B	Tom Tellmann
1692	8-02-84	Milwaukee	1B	Bob McClure
1693	8-03-84	Cleveland (1)	1B	Steve Comer
1694	8-07-84	Chicago (1)	2B	LaMarr Hoyt
1695	8-07-84	Chicago (2)	1B	Jerry Don Gleaton
1696	8-07-84	Chicago (2)	HR	Dan Spillner
1697	8-09-84	Chicago	1B	Tom Seaver
1698	8-09-84	Chicago	1B	Tom Seaver
1699	8-09-84	Chicago	1B	Bert Roberge
1700	8-10-84	at Cleveland (1)	1B	Don Schulze

NO.	DATE	OPPONENT	HIT	PITCHER
1701	8-10-84	at Cleveland (2)	HR	Steve Comer
1702	8-10-84	at Cleveland (2)	1B	Steve Comer
1703	8-10-84	at Cleveland (2)	1B	Mike Jeffcoat
1704	8-11-84	at Cleveland	1B	Steve Farr
1705	8-11-84	at Cleveland	1B	Steve Farr
1706	8-11-84	at Cleveland	1B	Jamie Easterly
1707	8-12-84	at Cleveland	1B	Bert Blyleven
1708	8-13-84	at Cleveland	1B	Roy Smith
1709	8-15-84	Seattle	1B	Jim Beattie
1710	8-17-84	Oakland	1B	Bill Krueger
1711	8-17-84	Oakland	1B	Bill Krueger
1712	8-18-84	Oakland	1B	Steve McCatty
1713	8-19-84	Oakland	1B	Ray Burris
1714	8-19-84	Oakland	HR	Ray Burris
1715	8-19-84	Oakland	1B	Ray Burris
1716	8-19-84	Oakland	1B	Bill Caudill
1717	8-20-84	California	3B	Tommy John
1718	8-21-84	California	1B	Ron Romanick
1719	8-21-84	California	1B	Ron Romanick
1720	8-22-84	California	1B	Jim Slaton
1721	8-24-84	at Seattle	1B	Mark Langston
1722	8-25-84	at Seattle	2B	Jim Beattie
1723	8-25-84	at Seattle	1B	Dave Beard
1724	8-26-84	at Seattle	HR	Salome Barojas
1725	8-27-84	at Oakland	2B	Bill Krueger
1726	8-28-84	at Oakland	HR	Tim Conroy
1727	8-28-84	at Oakland	1B	Bill Caudill
1728	8-28-84	at Oakland	1B	Bill Caudill
1729	8-29-84	at Oakland	1B	Keith Atherton
1730	8-31-84	at California	1B	John Curtis
1731	9-01-84	at California	1B	Geoff Zahn
1732	9-02-84	at California	1B	Ron Romanick
1733	9-02-84	at California	2B	Ron Romanick
1734	9-03-84	Toronto	1B	Luis Leal
1735	9-03-84	Toronto	HR	Luis Leal
1736	9-04-84	Toronto	HR	Jim Clancy
1737	9-05-84	Toronto	1B	Dave Stieb
1738	9-07-84	at Boston	2B	Bob Ojeda
1739	9-07-84	at Boston	1B	Bob Ojeda
1740	9-07-84	at Boston	3B	Bob Ojeda
1741	9-08-84	at Boston	2B	Bruce Hurst
1742	9-10-84	at Toronto	1B	Ron Musselman
1743	9-11-84	at Toronto	HR	Dennis Lamp
1744	9-12-84	at Toronto	1B	Doyle Alexander
1745	9-13-84	at Toronto	1B	Luis Leal
1746	9-13-84	at Toronto	1B	Bryan Clark
1747	9-14-84	Boston	1B	Charlie Mitchell
1748	9-15-84	Boston	1B	Al Nipper
1749	9-15-84	Boston	2B	Al Nipper
1750	9-15-84	Boston	1B	Al Nipper
1751	9-16-84	Boston	2B	Oil Can Boyd
1752	9-22-84	at Detroit	1B	Dan Petry
1753	9-24-84	at Baltimore (1)	1B	Mike Boddicker
1754	9-24-84	at Baltimore (2)	1B	Bill Swaggerty
1755	9-25-84	at Baltimore	1B	Mike Flanagan
1756	9-25-84	at Baltimore	1B	Mike Flanagan
1757	9-26-84	at Baltimore	1B	Storm Davis
1758	9-28-84	Detroit	2B	Dan Petry
1759	9-28-84	Detroit	2B	Dan Petry
1760	9-29-84	Detroit	1B	Juan Berenguer
1761	9-30-84	Detroit	1B	Randy O'Neal
1762	4-10-85	at Boston	3B	Bruce Hurst
1763	4-10-85	at Boston	1B	Bruce Hurst
1764	4-11-85	at Boston	1B	Roger Clemens
1765	4-11-85	at Boston	1B	Roger Clemens
1766	4-11-85	at Boston	HR	Roger Clemens
1767	4-11-85	at Boston	1B	Bob Stanley
1768	4-16-85	Chicago	1B	Tim Lollar
1769	4-16-85	Chicago	HR	Gene Nelson
1770	4-20-85	Cleveland	1B	Jose Roman
1771	4-21-85	Cleveland	1B	Vern Ruhle
1772	4-23-85	Boston	1B	Oil Can Boyd
1773	4-25-85	Boston	2B	Bruce Hurst
1774	4-26-85	at Chicago	1B	Tom Seaver
1775	4-26-85	at Chicago	2B	Tom Seaver
1776	4-26-85	at Chicago	1B	Bob James
1777	4-27-85	at Chicago	1B	Juan Agosto
1778	4-29-85	at Texas	1B	Frank Tanana
1779	4-30-85	at Texas	1B	Dave Rozema
1780	5-03-85	Kansas City	2B	Danny Jackson
1781	5-05-85	Kansas City	1B	Bud Black
1782	5-10-85	at Kansas City	1B	Charlie Leibrandt
1783	5-10-85	at Kansas City	1B	Charlie Leibrandt
1784	5-11-85	at Kansas City	1B	Bud Black
1785	5-11-85	at Kansas City	1B	Mike LaCoss

▼ Dave won five of his seven Rawlings Gold Glove awards as a member of the Yankees.

New York Yankees

▲ As a member of the Yankees, Dave made his first World Series appearance versus the Los Angeles Dodgers in 1981.

New York Yankees

▲ Dave takes a lead during the 1987 season.

NO.	DATE	OPPONENT	HIT	PITCHER
1786	5-11-85	at Kansas City	3B	Mike Jones
1787	5-13-85	Minnesota	1B	Mike Smithson
1788	5-13-85	Minnesota	1B	Mike Smithson
1789	5-14-85	Minnesota	HR	Tom Klawitter
1790	5-15-85	Texas	1B	Mike Mason
1791	5-18-85	at California	1B	Tommy John
1792	5-19-85	at California	1B	Jim Slaton
1793	5-21-85	at Seattle	2B	Salome Barojas
1794	5-21-85	at Seattle	1B	Mike T. Stanton
1795	5-21-85	at Seattle	1B	Edwin Nunez
1796	5-22-85	at Seattle	2B	Matt Young
1797	5-23-85	at Seattle	1B	Jim Beattie
1798	5-24-85	at Oakland	HR	Tom Tellmann
1799	5-25-85	at Oakland	1B	Keith Atherton
1800	5-26-85	at Oakland	2B	Steve McCatty
1801	5-27-85	at Oakland	2B	Jay Howell
1802	5-29-85	California	2B	Jim Slaton
1803	5-30-85	California	1B	Ron Romanick
1804	5-31-85	Seattle	1B	Mark Langston
1805	5-31-85	Seattle	HR	Mark Langston
1806	5-31-85	Seattle	1B	Edwin Nunez
1807	6-01-85	Seattle	1B	Matt Young
1808	6-03-85	Oakland	1B	Chris Codiroli
1809	6-03-85	Oakland	1B	Chris Codiroli
1810	6-03-85	Oakland	2B	Chris Codiroli
1811	6-03-85	Oakland	1B	Chris Codiroli
1812	6-07-85	at Milwaukee	HR	Jaime Cocanower
1813	6-07-85	at Milwaukee	HR	Bob McClure
1814	6-07-85	at Milwaukee	1B	Rollie Fingers
1815	6-08-85	at Milwaukee	1B	Ray Burris
1816	6-08-85	at Milwaukee	1B	Bob L. Gibson
1817	6-09-85	at Milwaukee	1B	Ray Searage
1818	6-10-85	Toronto	1B	Doyle Alexander
1819	6-10-85	Toronto	1B	Doyle Alexander
1820	6-10-85	Toronto	1B	Bill Caudill
1821	6-12-85	Toronto	1B	Gary Lavelle
1822	6-14-85	Detroit	1B	Walt Terrell
1823	6-16-85	Detroit	1B	Randy O'Neal
1824	6-17-85	at Baltimore	1B	Don Aase
1825	6-17-85	at Baltimore	1B	Tippy Martinez
1826	6-17-85	at Baltimore	1B	Dennis Martinez
1827	6-19-85	at Baltimore	1B	Ken Dixon
1828	6-19-85	at Baltimore	HR	Ken Dixon
1829	6-19-85	at Baltimore	1B	Sammy Stewart
1830	6-20-85	at Detroit	1B	Jack Morris
1831	6-20-85	at Detroit	1B	Jack Morris
1832	6-20-85	at Detroit	1B	Aurelio Lopez
1833	6-22-85	at Detroit	1B	Dan Petry
1834	6-22-85	at Detroit	2B	Dan Petry
1835	6-23-85	at Detroit	1B	Frank Tanana
1836	6-23-85	at Detroit	1B	Frank Tanana
1837	6-24-85	Baltimore	2B	Dennis Martinez
1838	6-24-85	Baltimore	1B	Dennis Martinez
1839	6-26-85	Baltimore	1B	Scott McGregor
1840	6-28-85	Milwaukee	HR	Danny Darwin
1841	6-30-85	Milwaukee	1B	Ray Burris
1842	6-30-85	Milwaukee	1B	Ray Burris
1843	7-02-85	at Toronto	1B	Bill Caudill
1844	7-03-85	at Toronto	2B	Dave Stieb
1845	7-03-85	at Toronto	1B	Dave Stieb
1846	7-03-85	at Toronto	1B	Gary Lavelle
1847	7-07-85	Minnesota (1)	2B	Mike Smithson
1848	7-07-85	Minnesota (1)	HR	Curt Wardle
1849	7-07-85	Minnesota (2)	1B	Rick Lysander
1850	7-07-85	Minnesota (2)	1B	Mark Brown
1851	7-07-85	Minnesota (2)	1B	Mark Brown
1852	7-09-85	Kansas City	1B	Bud Black
1853	7-10-85	Kansas City	2B	Mark Gubicza
1854	7-10-85	Kansas City	1B	Dan Quisenberry
1855	7-11-85	Texas	HR	Glen Cook
1856	7-11-85	Texas	1B	Dave Rozema
1857	7-13-85	Texas	1B	Mike Mason
1858	7-13-85	Texas	1B	Dave Schmidt
1859	7-14-85	Texas	HR	Burt Hooton
1860	7-18-85	at Minnesota	2B	Mike Smithson
1861	7-19-85	at Minnesota	1B	John Butcher
1862	7-19-85	at Minnesota	1B	Ron Davis
1863	7-20-85	at Minnesota	2B	Ken Schrom
1864	7-21-85	at Minnesota	HR	Frank Viola
1865	7-22-85	at Kansas City	2B	Mark Gubicza
1866	7-22-85	at Kansas City	3B	Mark Gubicza
1867	7-28-85	at Texas	1B	Chris Welch
1868	7-28-85	at Texas	1B	Chris Welch
1869	7-29-85	at Cleveland	2B	Bert Blyleven
1870	7-29-85	at Cleveland	HR	Bert Blyleven

Those fortunate enough to see Winfield regularly during those years could appreciate what Martin meant. Game after game, year after year, he put up numbers and, despite what that lone critic kept saying, would so often come through with the game on the line. The memories of Winfield's heroics become a collage of highlight-film moments: An upper-deck homer to left field in the ninth inning that beat Oakland, a mad dash around the bases to score from first with the game-winning run against Texas, a trek through the rain-drenched outfield in

◀ Dave and Don Mattingly were teammates from 1982 to 1990.

Baltimore to rob Eddie Murray of what would have been a game-winning homer.

Winfield was a clubhouse presence with the Yankees as well. It was Winfield who would get on Rickey Henderson — sometimes good-naturedly, sometimes sternly — when the temperamental star would go into one of his funks. "Dave Winfield is a man's man," teammate Don Baylor once said. "As a player and as a person, he's right there."

Winfield's interests went far beyond the boundaries of the game, as his work with the Winfield Foundation and numerous other community service ventures showed. In addition, he also knew how to deal with people. Remember the infamous incident in Toronto in 1983, when he accidentally killed a seagull with a between-innings warm-up throw at old Exhibition Stadium?

Winfield was arrested after the game, charged with cruelty to animals, and briefly became Canada's most notorious villain. But he treated the situation with class, making a charitable donation and an off-season appearance in Toronto, and quickly became a hero — many years before his 1992 heroics as a member of the Blue Jays, capped by his game-winning hit in the sixth and final World Series game.

That Series-winning hit helped Winfield forget the horrible memory of his only previous appearance in the Fall Classic, with the 1981 Yankees. He went 1-for-22 in that Series, as the Yankees lost to the Dodgers in six games. Following the post-season, Winfield was ridiculed by Steinbrenner, who said, "Winfield isn't the winner the way Reggie Jackson is. He can't carry a team the way Reggie did when it counts."

Nobody around the Yankees during the Winfield years would agree with that. But the Steinbrenner-Winfield relationship had become the dominant theme of those years.

Managers learned to expect calls from Steinbrenner, with "suggestions" that Winfield be benched against right-handers. One of those managers was Lou Piniella, a teammate of Winfield's for four

NO.	DATE	OPPONENT	HIT	PITCHER
1871	7-30-85	at Cleveland (1)	1B	Neal Heaton
1872	7-30-85	at Cleveland (1)	HR	Neal Heaton
1873	7-31-85	at Cleveland	1B	Tom Waddell
1874	7-31-85	at Cleveland	1B	Tom Waddell
1875	8-02-85	Chicago	HR	Mike T. Stanton
1876	8-05-85	Chicago	2B	Floyd Bannister
1877	8-08-85	Cleveland (1)	HR	Curt Wardle
1878	8-08-85	Cleveland (1)	HR	Curt Wardle
1879	8-08-85	Cleveland(1)	1B	Bryan Clark
1880	8-09-85	at Boston	1B	Bob Stanley
1881	8-09-85	at Boston	2B	Bob Stanley
1882	8-10-85	at Boston	2B	Oil Can Boyd
1883	8-11-85	at Boston	3B	Steve Crawford
1884	8-11-85	at Boston	2B	Steve Crawford
1885	8-16-85	Boston	2B	Oil Can Boyd
1886	8-16-85	Boston	2B	Steve Crawford
1887	8-17-85	Boston	3B	Al Nipper
1888	8-19-85	Boston	HR	Bruce Hurst
1889	8-19-85	Boston	1B	Mark Clear
1890	8-20-85	at California	HR	Jim Slaton
1891	8-21-85	at California	2B	John Candelaria
1892	8-22-85	at California	1B	Mike Witt
1893	8-22-85	at California	1B	Mike Witt
1894	8-23-85	at Seattle	1B	Bill Swift
1895	8-23-85	at Seattle	HR	Bill Swift
1896	8-25-85	at Seattle	1B	Mike Moore
1897	8-26-85	at Oakland	1B	Chris Codiroli
1898	8-26-85	at Oakland	1B	Chris Codiroli
1899	8-29-85	California	1B	Kirk McCaskill
1900	9-02-85	Seattle	HR	Frank Wills
1901	9-03-85	Seattle	1B	Bill Swift
1902	9-03-85	Seattle	2B	Roy Thomas
1903	9-06-85	Oakland	1B	Steve Ontiveros
1904	9-06-85	Oakland	1B	Bill Krueger
1905	9-07-85	Oakland	2B	Tommy John
1906	9-07-85	Oakland	2B	Tommy John
1907	9-08-85	Oakland	HR	Rick Langford
1908	9-08-85	Oakland	1B	Steve Mura
1909	9-09-85	at Milwaukee	HR	Moose Haas
1910	9-10-85	at Milwaukee	1B	Ray Burris
1911	9-11-85	at Milwaukee	3B	Ted Higuera
1912	9-12-85	at Toronto	1B	Dave Stieb
1913	9-12-85	at Toronto	1B	Dennis Lamp
1914	9-13-85	at Toronto	1B	Gary Lavelle
1915	9-15-85	at Toronto	1B	Doyle Alexander
1916	9-15-85	at Toronto	1B	Doyle Alexander
1917	9-16-85	Cleveland	1B	Vern Ruhle
1918	9-18-85	at Detroit	1B	Juan Berenguer
1919	9-18-85	at Detroit	1B	Mickey Mahler
1920	9-19-85	at Detroit	1B	Frank Tanana
1921	9-21-85	at Baltimore	1B	Storm Davis
1922	9-21-85	at Baltimore	1B	Dennis Martinez
1923	9-25-85	Detroit	2B	Jack Morris
1924	9-25-85	Detroit	1B	Jack Morris
1925	9-28-85	Baltimore	HR	Ken Dixon
1926	9-28-85	Baltimore	1B	Sammy Stewart
1927	9-29-85	Baltimore (1)	1B	John Habyan
1928	9-29-85	Baltimore (2)	2B	Brad Havens
1929	9-29-85	Baltimore (2)	1B	Brad Havens
1930	9-29-85	Baltimore (2)	HR	Brad Havens
1931	9-30-85	Baltimore	2B	Mike Flanagan
1932	9-30-85	Baltimore	2B	Don Aase
1933	10-1-85	Milwaukee	2B	Bob McClure
1934	10-2-85	Milwaukee	2B	Ted Higuera
1935	10-5-85	at Toronto	1B	Doyle Alexander
1936	4-10-86	Kansas City	3B	Bret Saberhagen
1937	4-12-86	Milwaukee	HR	Ted Higuera
1938	4-15-86	at Cleveland	1B	Tom Candiotti
1939	4-15-86	at Cleveland	1B	Jamie Easterly
1940	4-15-86	at Cleveland	2B	Jim Kern
1941	4-17-86	at Cleveland	2B	Phil Niekro
1942	4-18-86	at Milwaukee	2B	Bill Wegman
1943	4-19-86	at Milwaukee	2B	Ted Higuera
1944	4-20-86	at Milwaukee	2B	Mark Clear
1945	4-21-86	at Kansas City	1B	Bret Saberhagen
1946	4-21-86	at Kansas City	1B	Danny Jackson
1947	4-22-86	at Kansas City	1B	Mark Gubicza
1948	4-23-86	at Kansas City	1B	Danny Jackson
1949	4-25-86	Cleveland	1B	Rich Yett
1950	4-26-86	Cleveland	1B	Don Schulze
1951	4-26-86	Cleveland	1B	Don Schulze
1952	4-27-86	Cleveland	1B	Phil Niekro
1953	4-27-86	Cleveland	1B	Phil Niekro
1954	4-27-86	Cleveland	1B	Phil Niekro
1955	4-30-86	Minnesota	2B	Bert Blyleven

MAJOR LEAGUE BASEBALL

NO.	DATE	OPPONENT	HIT	PITCHER
1956	5-01-86	Minnesota	HR	Frank Viola
1957	5-03-86	Texas	2B	Dwayne Henry
1958	5-03-86	Texas	2B	Greg A. Harris
1959	5-04-86	Texas	1B	Mike Mason
1960	5-06-86	at Chicago	1B	Dave Schmidt
1961	5-11-86	at Texas (2)	1B	Jose Guzman
1962	5-13-86	at Minnesota	1B	Bert Blyleven
1963	5-13-86	at Minnesota	HR	Bert Blyleven
1964	5-16-86	Seattle	3B	Mark Langston
1965	5-17-86	Seattle	2B	Matt Young
1966	5-17-86	Seattle	HR	Matt Young
1967	5-17-86	Seattle	1B	Bill Swift
1968	5-18-86	Seattle	1B	Lee Guetterman
1969	5-18-86	Seattle	1B	Lee Guetterman
1970	5-20-86	Oakland	2B	Curt Young
1971	5-22-86	Oakland	HR	Joaquin Andujar
1972	5-22-86	Oakland	2B	Jay Howell
1973	5-23-86	California	1B	Don Sutton
1974	5-24-86	California	HR	Donnie Moore
1975	5-31-86	at Oakland	HR	Eric Plunk
1976	6-01-86	at Oakland	1B	Dave Stewart
1977	6-01-86	at Oakland	HR	Dave Leiper
1978	6-02-86	at California	1B	Jim Slaton
1979	6-04-86	at California	HR	Ron Romanick
1980	6-04-86	at California	HR	Ron Romanick
1981	6-06-86	Baltimore	1B	Don Aase
1982	6-08-86	Baltimore	2B	Ken Dixon
1983	6-08-86	Baltimore	3B	Tippy Martinez
1984	6-10-86	at Detroit	1B	Walt Terrell
1985	6-11-86	at Detroit	HR	Frank Tanana
1986	6-12-86	at Baltimore	1B	Don Aase
1987	6-13-86	at Baltimore	1B	Storm Davis
1988	6-14-86	at Baltimore	HR	Scott McGregor
1989	6-17-86	Boston	1B	Steve Crawford
1990	6-22-86	at Toronto	1B	Jimmy Key
1991	6-23-86	at Boston	2B	Oil Can Boyd
1992	6-23-86	at Boston	2B	Oil Can Boyd
1993	6-23-86	at Boston	1B	Steve Crawford
1994	6-28-86	Toronto	1B	Jimmy Key
1995	6-29-86	Toronto	1B	Dave Stieb
1996	6-30-86	Detroit	1B	Walt Terrell
1997	7-02-86	Detroit	2B	Dave LaPoint
1998	7-06-86	at Chicago	HR	Floyd Bannister
1999	7-06-86	at Chicago	2B	Bob James
2000	7-07-86	at Texas	3B	Mickey Mahler
2001	7-07-86	at Texas	2B	Jeff Russell
2002	7-08-86	at Texas	1B	Mike Mason
2003	7-09-86	at Texas	2B	Mitch Williams
2004	7-10-86	at Minnesota	1B	Frank Viola
2005	7-10-86	at Minnesota	1B	Frank Pastore
2006	7-18-86	Chicago	1B	Floyd Bannister
2007	7-18-86	Chicago	1B	Dave Schmidt
2008	7-19-86	Chicago	2B	Joe Cowley
2009	7-20-86	Chicago	1B	Neil Allen
2010	7-21-86	Texas	1B	Jeff Russell
2011	7-22-86	Texas	HR	Edwin Correa
2012	7-22-86	Texas	2B	Edwin Correa
2013	7-22-86	Texas	1B	Jeff Russell
2014	7-25-86	Minnesota	1B	Keith Atherton
2015	7-25-86	Minnesota	HR	Keith Atherton
2016	7-26-86	Minnesota	1B	Allan Anderson
2017	7-26-86	Minnesota	1B	Allan Anderson
2018	7-28-86	at Milwaukee	1B	Juan Nieves
2019	7-29-86	at Milwaukee	1B	Danny Darwin
2020	7-29-86	at Milwaukee	1B	Danny Darwin
2021	7-29-86	at Milwaukee	HR	Danny Darwin
2022	7-30-86	at Milwaukee	1B	Ted Higuera
2023	8-02-86	at Cleveland	1B	Ernie Camacho
2024	8-03-86	at Cleveland	1B	Frank Wills
2025	8-04-86	Milwaukee	1B	Ted Higuera
2026	8-06-86	Milwaukee	1B	Juan Nieves
2027	8-06-86	Milwaukee	HR	Juan Nieves
2028	8-06-86	Milwaukee	1B	Bryan Clutterbuck
2029	8-07-86	Milwaukee	2B	Tim Leary
2030	8-07-86	Milwaukee	1B	Tim Leary
2031	8-07-86	Milwaukee	2B	John Henry Johnson
2032	8-08-86	Kansas City	1B	Charlie Leibrandt
2033	8-09-86	Kansas City	1B	Steve Farr
2034	8-10-86	Kansas City	2B	Scott Bankhead
2035	8-10-86	Kansas City	2B	Scott Bankhead
2036	8-10-86	Kansas City	1B	Dennis Leonard
2037	8-11-86	Cleveland	1B	Phil Niekro
2038	8-11-86	Cleveland	1B	Phil Niekro
2039	8-15-86	at Kansas City	1B	Dan Quisenberry
2040	8-16-86	at Kansas City	HR	Danny Jackson

▼ Dave was an All-Star in each of his first eight seasons as a Yankee.

seasons in New York before taking over as the Yankees skipper for two terms from 1986-88. "It's a no-win situation," Piniella said at the time. "If I play Winfield, I'm in trouble with Steinbrenner. If I don't play him I lose the respect of the team because everyone will know why I'm not playing him. And we need Winfield in the lineup. So I know this will get me fired, but as long as I'm the manager he's playing." Piniella was fired after the season.

Winfield's years with the Yankees could have been, and should have been different. Because, as Don Mattingly once said, "Dave Winfield was a great player for us, a great Yankee." 🎾

▼ Dave missed the entire 1989 season with the Yankees due to a back injury.

Otto Greule Jr./Allsport USA

NO.	DATE	OPPONENT	HIT	PITCHER
2041	8-20-86	Seattle	HR	Mike Moore
2042	8-20-86	Seattle	1B	Mike Moore
2043	8-20-86	Seattle	1B	Lee Guetterman
2044	8-22-86	Oakland	1B	Joaquin Andujar
2045	8-24-86	Oakland	1B	Dave Stewart
2046	8-28-86	at Seattle	1B	Mike Morgan
2047	8-28-86	at Seattle	1B	Mike Morgan
2048	8-29-86	at Seattle	2B	Karl Best
2049	8-29-86	at Seattle	1B	Karl Best
2050	8-30-86	at Seattle (1)	1B	Bill Swift
2051	8-31-86	at Seattle	1B	Mike Moore
2052	8-31-86	at Seattle	1B	Mike Moore
2053	9-02-86	at Oakland	HR	Curt Young
2054	9-02-86	at Oakland	1B	Bill Mooneyham
2055	9-11-86	at Toronto (1)	2B	Jimmy Key
2056	9-11-86	at Toronto (2)	2B	John Cerutti
2057	9-11-86	at Toronto (2)	1B	John Cerutti
2058	9-11-86	at Toronto (2)	1B	Tom Henke
2059	9-12-86	Boston	1B	Bruce Hurst
2060	9-13-86	Boston	HR	Sammy Stewart
2061	9-14-86	Boston	1B	Al Nipper
2062	9-15-86	Baltimore	1B	Mike Boddicker
2063	9-16-86	Baltimore	HR	Nate Snell
2064	9-17-86	Baltimore	2B	Eric Bell
2065	9-19-86	at Detroit	2B	Dan Petry
2066	9-19-86	at Detroit	1B	Mark Thurmond
2067	9-21-86	at Detroit	1B	Walt Terrell
2068	9-22-86	at Baltimore	1B	Scott McGregor
2069	9-23-86	at Baltimore	1B	Eric Bell
2070	9-23-86	at Baltimore	HR	Eric Bell
2071	9-23-86	at Baltimore	1B	Rich Bordi
2072	9-24-86	at Baltimore	1B	Mike Flanagan
2073	9-26-86	Detroit	1B	Eric King
2074	9-28-86	Detroit	1B	Bryan Kelly
2075	9-28-86	Detroit	HR	Mark Thurmond
2076	9-28-86	Detroit	1B	Jim Slaton
2077	9-29-86	Toronto	1B	Bill Caudill
2078	9-30-86	Toronto	1B	Dave Stieb
2079	9-30-86	Toronto	1B	Mark Eichhorn
2080	10-2-86	at Boston	1B	Bruce Hurst
2081	10-2-86	at Boston	3B	Sammy Stewart
2082	10-2-86	at Boston	2B	Joe Sambito
2083	10-4-86	at Boston (1)	2B	Oil Can Boyd
2084	4-06-87	at Detroit	1B	Jack Morris
2085	4-08-87	at Detroit	1B	Dan Petry
2086	4-09-87	at Detroit	1B	Walt Terrell
2087	4-09-87	at Detroit	1B	Walt Terrell
2088	4-11-87	at Kansas City	1B	Danny Jackson
2089	4-11-87	at Kansas City	1B	Dave Gumpert
2090	4-12-87	at Kansas City	1B	Charlie Leibrandt
2091	4-12-87	at Kansas City	1B	Dan Quisenberry
2092	4-13-87	Cleveland	HR	Greg Swindell
2093	4-13-87	Cleveland	2B	Ed VandeBerg
2094	4-15-87	Cleveland	1B	Scott Bailes
2095	4-15-87	Cleveland	1B	Ernie Camacho
2096	4-18-87	Kansas City	2B	Danny Jackson
2097	4-19-87	Kansas City (1)	1B	Charlie Leibrandt
2098	4-19-87	Kansas City (1)	1B	Dave Gumpert
2099	4-19-87	Kansas City (1)	1B	Dave Gumpert
2100	4-19-87	Kansas City (2)	1B	Mark Gubicza
2101	4-20-87	Detroit	1B	Jack Morris
2102	4-20-87	Detroit	1B	Mark Thurmond
2103	4-21-87	Detroit	1B	Walt Terrell
2104	4-23-87	at Cleveland	HR	Greg Swindell
2105	4-23-87	at Cleveland	HR	Greg Swindell
2106	4-26-87	at Cleveland	1B	Tom Candiotti
2107	4-26-87	at Cleveland	HR	Ed VandeBerg
2108	4-26-87	at Cleveland	1B	Doug Jones
2109	5-02-87	at Minnesota	HR	Frank Viola
2110	5-02-87	at Minnesota	1B	Juan Berenguer
2111	5-04-87	at Chicago	3B	Richard Dotson
2112	5-06-87	at Chicago	2B	Floyd Bannister
2113	5-06-87	at Chicago	1B	Floyd Bannister
2114	5-08-87	Minnesota	2B	Mark Portugal
2115	5-09-87	Minnesota	1B	Les Straker
2116	5-11-87	Chicago	HR	Floyd Bannister
2117	5-12-87	Chicago	1B	Bill Long
2118	5-13-87	Texas	1B	Jose Guzman
2119	5-13-87	Texas	HR	Jose Guzman
2120	5-14-87	Texas	1B	Edwin Correa
2121	5-15-87	at Seattle	1B	Mike Morgan
2122	5-16-87	at Seattle	2B	Bill Wilkinson
2123	5-17-87	at Seattle	1B	Mike Moore
2124	5-18-87	at Oakland	HR	Curt Young
2125	5-18-87	at Oakland	HR	Curt Young

NO.	DATE	OPPONENT	HIT	PITCHER
2126	5-19-87	at Oakland	1B	Steve Ontiveros
2127	5-24-87	at California	1B	Don Sutton
2128	5-24-87	at California	1B	Don Sutton
2129	5-25-87	at California	1B	Jack Lazorko
2130	5-27-87	Seattle	HR	Scott Bankhead
2131	5-28-87	Seattle	HR	Mike Moore
2132	5-29-87	Oakland	1B	Curt Young
2133	5-31-87	Oakland	1B	Dennis Eckersley
2134	5-31-87	Oakland	2B	Dennis Eckersley
2135	6-03-87	California	1B	Chuck Finley
2136	6-05-87	at Milwaukee	2B	Juan Nieves
2137	6-05-87	at Milwaukee	2B	John Henry Johnson
2138	6-05-87	at Milwaukee	HR	Jay Aldrich
2139	6-06-87	at Milwaukee	1B	Bill Wegman
2140	6-06-87	at Milwaukee	HR	Dan Plesac
2141	6-10-87	Toronto	1B	Jimmy Key
2142	6-12-87	Milwaukee	1B	Chuck Crim
2143	6-15-87	Baltimore	1B	Eric Bell
2144	6-15-87	Baltimore	1B	John Habyan
2145	6-16-87	Baltimore	1B	Ken Dixon
2146	6-16-87	Baltimore	HR	Ken Dixon
2147	6-16-87	Baltimore	HR	Ken Dixon
2148	6-17-87	Baltimore	2B	Mike Boddicker
2149	6-17-87	Baltimore	1B	Mike Boddicker
2150	6-18-87	Baltimore	1B	Scott McGregor
2151	6-18-87	Baltimore	2B	Tony Arnold
2152	6-19-87	at Boston	1B	Bruce Hurst
2153	6-19-87	at Boston	1B	Calvin Schiraldi
2154	6-20-87	at Boston	2B	Al Nipper
2155	6-21-87	at Boston	2B	Roger Clemens
2156	6-22-87	at Baltimore	1B	Eric Bell
2157	6-23-87	at Baltimore	1B	Mark Williamson
2158	6-24-87	at Baltimore	1B	Dave Schmidt
2159	6-26-87	Boston	HR	Roger Clemens
2160	6-26-87	Boston	1B	Steve Crawford
2161	6-27-87	Boston	1B	Oil Can Boyd
2162	6-27-87	Boston	1B	Oil Can Boyd
2163	6-29-87	at Toronto	HR	John Cerutti
2164	6-29-87	at Toronto	HR	Tom Henke
2165	6-30-87	at Toronto	1B	David Wells
2166	6-30-87	at Toronto	1B	David Wells
2167	7-01-87	at Toronto	1B	Jimmy Key
2168	7-05-87	Texas	HR	Edwin Correa
2169	7-05-87	Texas	1B	Jeff Russell
2170	7-06-87	Minnesota	1B	Frank Viola
2171	7-07-87	Minnesota	1B	Dan Schatzeder
2172	7-09-87	Chicago	2B	Richard Dotson
2173	7-10-87	Chicago	1B	Scott Nielsen
2174	7-10-87	Chicago	HR	Joel McKeon
2175	7-11-87	Chicago	1B	Jose DeLeon
2176	7-11-87	Chicago	1B	Jim Winn
2177	7-12-87	Chicago	1B	Floyd Bannister
2178	7-19-87	at Texas	2B	Jeff Russell
2179	7-21-87	at Minnesota	1B	Bert Blyleven
2180	7-22-87	at Minnesota	1B	Frank Viola
2181	7-24-87	at Chicago	1B	Floyd Bannister
2182	7-25-87	at Chicago	1B	Neil Allen
2183	7-25-87	at Chicago	1B	Neil Allen
2184	7-26-87	at Chicago	HR	Richard Dotson
2185	7-28-87	Kansas City	1B	Mark Gubicza
2186	7-29-87	Kansas City	1B	Danny Jackson
2187	7-31-87	Detroit	2B	Walt Terrell
2188	8-02-87	Detroit	1B	Jeff M. Robinson
2189	8-02-87	Detroit	1B	Jeff M. Robinson
2190	8-02-87	Detroit	1B	Willie Hernandez
2191	8-04-87	at Cleveland	1B	Ken Schrom
2192	8-04-87	at Cleveland	HR	Ken Schrom
2193	8-06-87	at Detroit	1B	Frank Tanana
2194	8-07-87	at Detroit	1B	Jeff M. Robinson
2195	8-09-87	at Detroit	1B	Dan Petry
2196	8-10-87	at Kansas City	1B	Danny Jackson
2197	8-11-87	at Kansas City	1B	Bret Saberhagen
2198	8-11-87	at Kansas City	1B	Jerry Don Gleaton
2199	8-12-87	at Kansas City	2B	Charlie Leibrandt
2200	8-15-87	Cleveland	1B	Ken Schrom
2201	8-15-87	Cleveland	2B	Don Gordon
2202	8-22-87	at Oakland	1B	Gene Nelson
2203	8-22-87	at Oakland	1B	Gene Nelson
2204	8-22-87	at Oakland	1B	Greg Cadaret
2205	8-24-87	at California	HR	Don Sutton
2206	8-25-87	at California	1B	John Candelaria
2207	8-28-87	Seattle	2B	Dennis Powell
2208	8-28-87	Seattle	1B	Dennis Powell
2209	8-30-87	Seattle	1B	Mike Moore
2210	8-31-87	Oakland	1B	Curt Young

▲ A group of youngsters receives baseball instruction during Dave's tour of Japan in 1989.

▲ Dave stretches prior to a game.

▼ Winfield ranks eighth on the all-time Yankee home run list with 205.

NO.	DATE	OPPONENT	HIT	PITCHER
2211	9-04-87	California	HR	Chuck Finley
2212	9-04-87	California	1B	DeWayne Buice
2213	9-05-87	California	1B	Don Sutton
2214	9-05-87	California	1B	Willie Fraser
2215	9-06-87	California	1B	DeWayne Buice
2216	9-07-87	at Boston	1B	Bruce Hurst
2217	9-07-87	at Boston	2B	Bruce Hurst
2218	9-07-87	at Boston	1B	Bruce Hurst
2219	9-07-87	at Boston	1B	Calvin Schiraldi
2220	9-08-87	at Boston	1B	Wes Gardner
2221	9-09-87	at Boston	1B	Roger Clemens
2222	9-09-87	at Boston	1B	Roger Clemens
2223	9-11-87	at Toronto	1B	Mike Flanagan
2224	9-11-87	at Toronto	2B	Mike Flanagan
2225	9-11-87	at Toronto	1B	Mark Eichhorn
2226	9-12-87	at Toronto	1B	Jimmy Key
2227	9-13-87	at Toronto	HR	John Cerutti
2228	9-15-87	Milwaukee	1B	Juan Nieves
2229	9-17-87	Toronto	2B	Dave Stieb
2230	9-19-87	Toronto	1B	Mike Flanagan
2231	9-20-87	Toronto	1B	Jimmy Key
2232	9-22-87	at Milwaukee (1)	1B	Mark Clear
2233	9-22-87	at Milwaukee (2)	1B	Dan Plesac
2234	9-22-87	at Milwaukee (2)	1B	Jay Aldrich
2235	9-25-87	at Baltimore	HR	Mike Griffin
2236	9-26-87	at Baltimore	HR	Mike Boddicker
2237	9-28-87	Boston	1B	Bob Woodward
2238	9-28-87	Boston	2B	Wes Gardner
2239	9-30-87	Boston	1B	Roger Clemens
2240	10-3-87	Baltimore	1B	John Habyan
2241	10-4-87	Baltimore	1B	Jose Mesa
2242	4-05-88	Minnesota	1B	Frank Viola
2243	4-06-88	Minnesota	1B	Juan Berenguer
2244	4-08-88	Milwaukee	HR	Juan Nieves
2245	4-08-88	Milwaukee	1B	Juan Nieves
2246	4-08-88	Milwaukee	HR	Mark Clear
2247	4-09-88	Milwaukee	2B	Bill Wegman
2248	4-09-88	Milwaukee	1B	Bill Wegman
2249	4-10-88	Milwaukee	1B	Ted Higuera
2250	4-10-88	Milwaukee	1B	Chuck Crim
2251	4-11-88	at Toronto	2B	Mike Flanagan
2252	4-11-88	at Toronto	1B	David Wells
2253	4-12-88	at Toronto	1B	Jim Clancy
2254	4-12-88	at Toronto	2B	John Cerutti
2255	4-13-88	at Toronto	1B	Dave Stieb
2256	4-13-88	at Toronto	2B	Mark Eichhorn
2257	4-14-88	at Toronto	3B	Jimmy Key
2258	4-14-88	at Toronto	HR	Jimmy Key
2259	4-17-88	at Milwaukee	1B	Ted Higuera
2260	4-18-88	at Minnesota	1B	Bert Blyleven
2261	4-18-88	at Minnesota	1B	Tippy Martinez
2262	4-18-88	at Minnesota	HR	Tippy Martinez
2263	4-19-88	at Minnesota	1B	Joe Niekro
2264	4-20-88	at Minnesota	HR	Frank Viola
2265	4-22-88	Toronto	1B	Mike Flanagan
2266	4-23-88	Toronto	1B	John Cerutti
2267	4-23-88	Toronto	HR	John Cerutti
2268	4-24-88	Toronto	2B	Jim Clancy
2269	4-26-88	Kansas City	HR	Charlie Leibrandt
2270	4-27-88	Kansas City	1B	Mark Gubicza
2271	4-28-88	Kansas City	1B	Floyd Bannister
2272	4-29-88	Texas	1B	Charlie Hough
2273	4-29-88	Texas	1B	Charlie Hough
2274	4-30-88	Texas	1B	Bobby Witt
2275	5-01-88	Texas	1B	Paul Kilgus
2276	5-01-88	Texas	1B	Paul Kilgus
2277	5-01-88	Texas	1B	Paul Kilgus
2278	5-01-88	Texas	1B	Dale Mohorcic
2279	5-02-88	at Chicago	1B	John Davis
2280	5-02-88	at Chicago	1B	Bobby Thigpen
2281	5-03-88	at Chicago	1B	Dave LaPoint
2282	5-03-88	at Chicago	1B	Dave LaPoint
2283	5-04-88	at Kansas City	2B	Charlie Leibrandt
2284	5-04-88	at Kansas City	1B	Charlie Leibrandt
2285	5-04-88	at Kansas City	1B	Ted Power
2286	5-06-88	at Texas	1B	Paul Kilgus
2287	5-10-88	Chicago	1B	Ricky Horton
2288	5-10-88	Chicago	1B	John Pawlowski
2289	5-11-88	Chicago	1B	Jack McDowell
2290	5-11-88	Chicago	1B	Jack McDowell
2291	5-13-88	California	1B	Kirk McCaskill
2292	5-14-88	California	HR	Dan Petry
2293	5-15-88	California	HR	Willie Fraser
2294	5-16-88	Seattle	1B	Mike Moore
2295	5-20-88	Oakland	2B	Bob Welch

NO.	DATE	OPPONENT	HIT	PITCHER
2296	5-23-88	at California	1B	Greg Minton
2297	5-24-88	at California	2B	Kirk McCaskill
2298	5-24-88	at California	1B	Kirk McCaskill
2299	5-25-88	at California	HR	DeWayne Buice
2300	5-28-88	at Seattle	2B	Bill Swift
2301	5-28-88	at Seattle	1B	Bill Swift
2302	5-29-88	at Seattle	HR	Mike Campbell
2303	5-30-88	at Oakland	HR	Bob Welch
2304	5-31-88	at Oakland	1B	Steve Ontiveros
2305	5-31-88	at Oakland	2B	Steve Ontiveros
2306	5-31-88	at Oakland	1B	Todd Burns
2307	6-03-88	at Baltimore	1B	Jose Bautista
2308	6-03-88	at Baltimore	2B	Don Aase
2309	6-04-88	at Baltimore	1B	Mike Boddicker
2310	6-04-88	at Baltimore	1B	Dave Schmidt
2311	6-04-88	at Baltimore	1B	Doug Sisk
2312	6-06-88	Boston	1B	Bruce Hurst
2313	6-06-88	Boston	1B	Lee Smith
2314	6-08-88	Boston	1B	Roger Clemens
2315	6-10-88	Baltimore	1B	Mike Boddicker
2316	6-10-88	Baltimore	HR	Mike Boddicker
2317	6-11-88	Baltimore	1B	Jeff Ballard
2318	6-13-88	at Boston	2B	Roger Clemens
2319	6-13-88	at Boston	1B	Roger Clemens
2320	6-13-88	at Boston	2B	Roger Clemens
2321	6-15-88	at Boston	HR	Bruce Hurst
2322	6-18-88	at Cleveland	HR	Scott Bailes
2323	6-20-88	at Detroit	2B	Jeff M. Robinson
2324	6-21-88	at Detroit	2B	Jack Morris
2325	6-21-88	at Detroit	1B	Eric King
2326	6-22-88	at Detroit	1B	Frank Tanana
2327	6-23-88	Cleveland	2B	Scott Bailes
2328	6-23-88	Cleveland	2B	Scott Bailes
2329	6-23-88	Cleveland	1B	Jon Perlman
2330	6-25-88	Cleveland	2B	Greg Swindell
2331	6-25-88	Cleveland	1B	Greg Swindell
2332	6-25-88	Cleveland	2B	Jon Perlman
2333	6-27-88	Detroit	1B	Jack Morris
2334	6-28-88	Detroit	2B	Frank Tanana
2335	6-30-88	at Chicago	1B	Joel Davis
2336	7-02-88	at Chicago	1B	Jerry Reuss
2337	7-03-88	at Chicago	1B	Bill Long
2338	7-03-88	at Chicago	1B	Bobby Thigpen
2339	7-03-88	at Chicago	1B	Jeff Bittiger
2340	7-04-88	at Texas	1B	DeWayne Vaughn
2341	7-05-88	at Texas	3B	Craig McMurtry
2342	7-06-88	at Texas	1B	Jeff Russell
2343	7-06-88	at Texas	2B	Jeff Russell
2344	7-10-88	Kansas City	1B	Rick Anderson
2345	7-15-88	Chicago	1B	Joel Davis
2346	7-16-88	Chicago	1B	Melido Perez
2347	7-17-88	Chicago	1B	Dave LaPoint
2348	7-17-88	Chicago	1B	Dave LaPoint
2349	7-17-88	Chicago	2B	Joel Davis
2350	7-21-88	at Kansas City	1B	Mark Gubicza
2351	7-23-88	at Kansas City	HR	Floyd Bannister
2352	7-23-88	at Kansas City	HR	Floyd Bannister
2353	7-23-88	at Kansas City	2B	Rick Anderson
2354	7-24-88	at Kansas City	1B	Bret Saberhagen
2355	7-25-88	Milwaukee	2B	Ted Higuera
2356	7-26-88	Milwaukee	1B	Don August
2357	7-27-88	Milwaukee	HR	Chris Bosio
2358	7-27-88	Milwaukee	1B	Chris Bosio
2359	7-27-88	Milwaukee	HR	Chuck Crim
2360	7-28-88	Milwaukee	1B	Mike Birkbeck
2361	7-29-88	at Toronto	1B	Jeff Musselman
2362	7-29-88	at Toronto	1B	Jeff Musselman
2363	7-30-88	at Toronto	HR	Tom Henke
2364	7-31-88	at Toronto	1B	Jimmy Key
2365	7-31-88	at Toronto	1B	Jimmy Key
2366	7-31-88	at Toronto	1B	Jimmy Key
2367	8-10-88	Toronto	1B	Jimmy Key
2368	8-10-88	Toronto	1B	Jimmy Key
2369	8-11-88	Toronto	1B	John Cerutti
2370	8-14-88	at Minnesota	2B	Fred Toliver
2371	8-14-88	at Minnesota	1B	German Gonzalez
2372	8-16-88	California	HR	Willie Fraser
2373	8-17-88	California	HR	Terry Clark
2374	8-17-88	California	2B	Terry Clark
2375	8-17-88	California	1B	Terry Clark
2376	8-17-88	California	1B	DeWayne Buice
2377	8-18-88	California	1B	Chuck Finley
2378	8-18-88	California	HR	Chuck Finley
2379	8-19-88	Seattle (1)	2B	Terry Taylor
2380	8-19-88	Seattle (1)	1B	Mike Schooler

▼ Taking the extra base!

▼ Dave sports Yankee pinstripes for the first time at spring training, 1981, in Fort Lauderdale, Fla.

Ken Griffey, Sr., on Winfield
Ken Griffey, Sr., Dave's New York Yankee teammate from 1982-86.

Hard work, personal pride and longevity, that's what comes to mind when I think about Dave Winfield. Playing with Dave in New York was a privilege for me because I learned how one person can rub off on others and make them want to do their best because he goes out and plays hard every day. He's done that for twenty years now and I watched him do it for five of them. I enjoyed playing with Dave and being around him because he's a very intelligent individual, but most importantly, because he's a fighter. During his ten years in New York he fought like heck just to stay there. He wanted to stay in New York and end his career as a Yankee. I can't tell you how much I admire Dave Winfield.

▼ A quiet moment in Cleveland Stadium.

NO.	DATE	OPPONENT	HIT	PITCHER
2381	8-21-88	Seattle	1B	Scott Bankhead
2382	8-22-88	Oakland	2B	Curt Young
2383	8-22-88	Oakland	1B	Gene Nelson
2384	8-23-88	Oakland	1B	Bob Welch
2385	8-24-88	Oakland	1B	Dave Stewart
2386	8-24-88	Oakland	1B	Dennis Eckersley
2387	8-24-88	Oakland	1B	Dennis Eckersley
2388	8-26-88	at California	1B	Willie Fraser
2389	8-26-88	at California	2B	Sherman Corbett
2390	8-28-88	at California	HR	DeWayne Buice
2391	8-29-88	at Seattle	1B	Mark Langston
2392	8-29-88	at Seattle	1B	Mike Schooler
2393	8-30-88	at Seattle	2B	Mike Campbell
2394	8-31-88	at Seattle	2B	Scott Bankhead
2395	8-31-88	at Seattle	1B	Scott Bankhead
2396	8-31-88	at Seattle	1B	Bill Swift
2397	9-03-88	at Oakland	1B	Eric Plunk
2398	9-04-88	at Oakland	1B	Dave Stewart
2399	9-05-88	Cleveland	1B	Tom Candiotti
2400	9-05-88	Cleveland	1B	Tom Candiotti
2401	9-05-88	Cleveland	1B	Jeff Dedmon
2402	9-07-88	Cleveland	1B	Rod Nichols
2403	9-07-88	Cleveland	1B	Doug Jones
2404	9-08-88	Detroit	1B	Ted Power
2405	9-10-88	Detroit	1B	Don Heinkel
2406	9-11-88	Detroit	2B	Doyle Alexander
2407	9-11-88	Detroit	2B	Doyle Alexander
2408	9-11-88	Detroit	1B	Mike Henneman
2409	9-13-88	at Cleveland	1B	Rod Nichols
2410	9-13-88	at Cleveland	2B	Rod Nichols
2411	9-13-88	at Cleveland	1B	Don Gordon
2412	9-14-88	at Cleveland	HR	Rich Yett
2413	9-14-88	at Cleveland	1B	Brad Havens
2414	9-14-88	at Cleveland	2B	Brad Havens
2415	9-15-88	at Boston	1B	Roger Clemens
2416	9-16-88	at Boston	2B	Dennis Lamp
2417	9-18-88	at Boston	2B	Mike Smithson
2418	9-19-88	Baltimore	1B	Pete Harnisch
2419	9-19-88	Baltimore	1B	Pete Harnisch
2420	9-24-88	Boston	1B	Mike Boddicker
2421	9-24-88	Boston	1B	Mike Boddicker
2422	4-12-90	Cleveland	2B	Bud Black
2423	4-13-90	Texas	1B	Bobby Witt
2424	4-13-90	Texas	2B	Mike Jeffcoat
2425	4-17-90	at Detroit	1B	Frank Tanana
2426	4-19-90	at Cleveland	1B	Doug Jones
2427	4-21-90	at Texas	HR	Charlie Hough
2428	4-21-90	at Texas	HR	Charlie Hough
2429	4-22-90	at Texas	1B	Kevin Brown
2430	4-22-90	at Texas	1B	Kevin Brown
2431	5-04-90	at California	1B	Mark Langston
2432	5-04-90	at California	1B	Mark Langston
2433	5-06-90	at California	1B	Mike Witt
2434	5-07-90	at Oakland	2B	Rick Honeycutt

"All Out" at 39

BY EARL BLOOM
ORANGE COUNTY REGISTER

Measured against the scope of his long and distinguished career — which is still very much a going enterprise — Dave Winfield's stay with the California Angels was brief. In not quite two full seasons in Anaheim, however, Winfield not only successfully revived a career threatened by a serious injury, he celebrated some significant milestones.

During the second year, 1991, he moved past such names as Babe Ruth, Joe DiMaggio, Al Simmons, Willie McCovey, Johnny Bench and Duke Snider on various career charts. And Angels' fans, who have grown used to Hall of Fame-bound performers passing through on their way to Cooperstown, were treated to a full measure of Winfield's class, which is as imposing as his physique.

"This guy brings a little more to the party," Angels manager Doug Rader said, upon Winfield's acquisition from the New York Yankees on May 11, 1990. "He has a presence."

A leader by example, by deed much more so than words, Winfield quickly introduced his all-out, all-the-time playing style to an Angels club that had often been accused of being too laid-back and willing to accept fate, rather than dare to determine it.

It is a measure of the way the man played the game that, although Winfield delivered such historical highlights as his 400th home run and hitting for the cycle, at age 39, while in an Angels uniform, one memory that stands out is a night he ran into an out.

Just eight days after the Angels rescued him from the Yankees, in exchange for right-hander Mike Witt, Winfield helped the Angels win an 11-9 SkyDome slugfest from the Blue Jays with a home run, two singles and two RBI. The homer, an opposite-field shot off David Wells in the top of the ninth, provided insurance that was nearly needed when the Angels bullpen struggled in the bottom of the inning.

But, of much more long-standing consequence was the assurance Winfield delivered in the third inning, when he tried — and failed — to hustle a single into a double. Junior Felix's perfect throw from right field cut him down, but anyone looking for statements could clearly read into Winfield's bold gamble: He was not worried about the back surgery that had sidelined him the previous season, threatening his career at age 38.

Winfield still intended to play the game the way he did when he walked off the University of Minnesota campus and into the San Diego Padres lineup in 1973: All out.

"To be that aggressive, it takes courage," Rader said. "That type of behavior become contagious. It takes someone to set an example. Whether it's leadership or whatever you want to call it, Dave Winfield brings it. That's why he was important to us."

Rader was one of those first-hand witnesses who got to share in Winnie's biggest moments as an Angel.

The first was his three-homer game April 13, 1991, in the Metrodome, a fitting venue for such a feat by the St. Paul native. Twins fans threw his first two home run balls

Earl Bloom is a staff writer for the Orange County Register. Bloom covered Dave Winfield as a member of the California Angels from 1990-1991.

NO.	DATE	OPPONENT	HIT	PITCHER
2435	5-18-90	at Toronto	1B	Dave Stieb
2436	5-19-90	at Toronto	1B	John Cerutti
2437	5-19-90	at Toronto	1B	John Cerutti
2438	5-19-90	at Toronto	HR	David Wells
2439	5-20-90	at Toronto	1B	Frank Wills
2440	5-21-90	at Cleveland	1B	Jeff Shaw
2441	5-24-90	Toronto	1B	David Wells
2442	5-25-90	Milwaukee	HR	Chris Bosio
2443	5-27-90	Milwaukee	1B	Bill Wegman
2444	5-28-90	Cleveland	1B	Bud Black
2445	6-02-90	at Texas	1B	Mike Jeffcoat
2446	6-05-90	at Kansas City	1B	Luis Aquino
2447	6-06-90	at Kansas City	HR	Tom Gordon
2448	6-08-90	Texas	2B	Charlie Hough
2449	6-08-90	Texas	HR	Charlie Hough
2450	6-09-90	Texas	2B	Jamie Moyer
2451	6-10-90	Texas	HR	Kevin Brown
2452	6-11-90	Kansas City	HR	Tom Gordon
2453	6-12-90	Kansas City	1B	Bret Saberhagen
2454	6-12-90	Kansas City	1B	Bret Saberhagen
2455	6-12-90	Kansas City	2B	Bret Saberhagen
2456	6-18-90	at Chicago	2B	Jack McDowell
2457	6-18-90	at Chicago	1B	Wayne Edwards
2458	6-19-90	at Chicago	1B	Melido Perez
2459	6-21-90	Detroit	HR	Jack Morris
2460	6-22-90	Detroit	3B	Paul Gibson
2461	6-23-90	Detroit	1B	Jerry Don Gleaton
2462	6-24-90	Detroit	2B	Frank Tanana
2463	6-27-90	Chicago	1B	Eric King
2464	6-27-90	Chicago	1B	Donn Pall
2465	6-30-90	at Cleveland	1B	Tom Candiotti
2466	7-01-90	at Cleveland	1B	Greg Swindell
2467	7-01-90	at Cleveland	1B	Doug Jones
2468	7-02-90	at Cleveland	1B	Bud Black
2469	7-02-90	at Cleveland	1B	Jesse Orosco
2470	7-03-90	at Toronto	1B	Todd Stottlemyre
2471	7-04-90	at Toronto	1B	John Cerutti
2472	7-05-90	at Toronto	2B	Dave Stieb
2473	7-06-90	at Milwaukee	HR	Jaime Navarro
2474	7-06-90	at Milwaukee	1B	Tom Edens
2475	7-14-90	Toronto	HR	John Cerutti
2476	7-14-90	Toronto	HR	Frank Wills
2477	7-16-90	Milwaukee	2B	Ron Robinson
2478	7-16-90	Milwaukee	1B	Ron Robinson
2479	7-17-90	Milwaukee	1B	Ted Higuera
2480	7-17-90	Milwaukee	1B	Ted Higuera
2481	7-18-90	Milwaukee	1B	Mark Knudson
2482	7-20-90	Cleveland	1B	Steve Olin
2483	7-21-90	Cleveland	2B	Mike Walker
2484	7-23-90	at Oakland	1B	Dave Stewart
2485	7-23-90	at Oakland	1B	Dave Stewart
2486	7-24-90	at Oakland	HR	Bob Welch
2487	7-30-90	at Minnesota	1B	Kevin Tapani
2488	7-30-90	at Minnesota	1B	Kevin Tapani
2489	7-31-90	at Minnesota	1B	Allan Anderson
2490	7-31-90	at Minnesota	1B	Allan Anderson

◄ Dave's home run in May of 1991 versus New York gave him at least one round-tripper against every team except San Diego.

V.J. LOVERO

▲ Headfirst against the White Sox in 1990.

back onto the field, but kept the third. "The fans really gave me a good response when I hit that third one," Winfield said. "I think they appreciated it. It was good to do it here."

His three homers, on his first three at-bats, added up to 1,200 feet. Winfield had five hits that night, and three chances to become the twelfth player to hit four homers, but while that was not to be, it would not be his last big night in Minnesota.

On June 24, outdoors this time at Kansas City but still on a carpeted surface, Winfield capped another five-hit night by hitting for the cycle with an eighth-inning triple off Royals infielder-turned-pitcher Bill Pecota.

"There are different days in your career that you're pleased, but you don't say much," said Winfield, who had reacted with the joy of a kid after trundling hard into third base. "I've done a lot of other things. It's a tough thing to do. Not many people do it. I'm just very pleased to accomplish it in a career."

Winfield moved back into the Metrodome for his next milestone, the 400th

homer, struck August 14, 1991, off David West. "It's like I wished," said Winfield, who shared a hug with brother Steve in the clubhouse afterward, and also had time for some Winniesque humor. "I'm glad to be off 399," he said, "it sounds like something you'd purchase at a discount store. This was good, to hit it here. This was where I first

▲ Dave teamed up with another veteran slugger,
Dave Parker, on the 1991 Angels.

▲ When Dave hit for the cycle against the Royals in 1991, he
became the oldest player in history to accomplish the feat.

NO.	DATE	OPPONENT	HIT	PITCHER
2491	7-31-90	at Minnesota	1B	Tim Drummond
2492	8-01-90	at Minnesota	1B	Roy Smith
2493	8-01-90	at Minnesota	1B	Juan Berenguer
2494	8-02-90	Oakland	1B	Bob Welch
2495	8-03-90	Oakland	1B	Scott Sanderson
2496	8-03-90	Oakland	HR	Reggie Harris
2497	8-03-90	Oakland	1B	Dennis Eckersley
2498	8-04-90	Oakland	2B	Todd Burns
2499	8-04-90	Oakland	1B	Joe Klink
2500	8-07-90	Boston	1B	Tom Bolton
2501	8-08-90	Boston	1B	Greg A. Harris
2502	8-09-90	Boston	2B	Joe Hesketh
2503	8-12-90	Baltimore	2B	John Mitchell
2504	8-12-90	Baltimore	1B	John Mitchell
2505	8-13-90	New York	1B	Greg Cadaret
2506	8-13-90	New York	2B	Greg Cadaret
2507	8-15-90	New York	1B	Dave LaPoint
2508	8-15-90	New York	1B	Dave LaPoint
2509	8-18-90	at Boston	1B	Tom Bolton
2510	8-19-90	at Boston	1B	Jeff Gray
2511	8-21-90	at Detroit	HR	Dan Petry
2512	8-21-90	at Detroit	1B	Edwin Nunez
2513	8-23-90	at Chicago	2B	Alex Fernandez
2514	8-24-90	at Chicago	2B	Wayne Edwards
2515	8-26-90	at Chicago	2B	Greg Hibbard
2516	8-26-90	at Chicago	1B	Greg Hibbard
2517	8-27-90	Texas	1B	John Barfield
2518	8-29-90	Texas	1B	Brad Arnsberg
2519	8-31-90	Chicago	1B	Bobby Thigpen
2520	9-06-90	at New York	3B	Chuck Cary
2521	9-06-90	at New York	1B	Lee Guetterman
2522	9-10-90	Minnesota	1B	Paul Abbott
2523	9-10-90	Minnesota	1B	Paul Abbott
2524	9-10-90	Minnesota	1B	Paul Abbott
2525	9-11-90	Minnesota	1B	Roy Smith
2526	9-11-90	Minnesota	HR	Roy Smith
2527	9-12-90	Minnesota	1B	Larry Casian
2528	9-12-90	Minnesota	1B	Tim Drummond
2529	9-14-90	Seattle	HR	Matt Young
2530	9-14-90	Seattle	HR	Matt Young
2531	9-15-90	Seattle	1B	Erik Hanson
2532	9-15-90	Seattle	HR	Erik Hanson
2533	9-19-90	Detroit	1B	Walt Terrell
2534	9-21-90	at Kansas City	2B	Bret Saberhagen
2535	9-21-90	at Kansas City	1B	Steve Crawford
2536	9-22-90	at Kansas City	1B	Hector Wagner
2537	9-22-90	at Kansas City	HR	Hector Wagner
2538	9-22-90	at Kansas City	1B	Andy McGaffigan
2539	9-25-90	at Texas	1B	Bobby Witt
2540	9-25-90	at Texas	1B	Bobby Witt
2541	9-25-90	at Texas	2B	Joe Bitker
2542	9-26-90	at Texas	1B	Kenny Rogers
2543	9-29-90	Kansas City	HR	Mark Davis
2544	9-30-90	Kansas City	1B	Kevin Appier
2545	10-1-90	at Oakland	2B	Dave Stewart
2546	10-2-90	at Oakland	1B	Gene Nelson
2547	10-3-90	at Oakland	1B	Mike Moore
2548	10-3-90	at Oakland	1B	Steve Chitren
2549	4-10-91	at Seattle	2B	Randy Johnson
2550	4-10-91	at Seattle	1B	Randy Johnson
2551	4-10-91	at Seattle	1B	Russ Swan
2552	4-11-91	at Seattle	2B	Bill Krueger
2553	4-13-91	at Minnesota	HR	Mark Guthrie
2554	4-13-91	at Minnesota	HR	Mark Guthrie
2555	4-13-91	at Minnesota	HR	Larry Casian
2556	4-13-91	at Minnesota	2B	Terry Leach
2557	4-13-91	at Minnesota	1B	Gary Wayne
2558	4-23-91	Seattle	1B	Scott Bankhead
2559	4-23-91	Seattle	2B	Scott Bankhead
2560	4-27-91	at Oakland	1B	Mike Moore
2561	4-28-91	at Oakland	1B	Dave Stewart
2562	5-01-91	Cleveland	1B	Tom Candiotti
2563	5-04-91	Baltimore	2B	Jeff M. Robinson
2564	5-05-91	Baltimore	1B	Jeff Ballard
2565	5-07-91	New York	HR	Andy Hawkins
2566	5-07-91	New York	1B	Andy Hawkins
2567	5-08-91	New York	1B	Scott Sanderson
2568	5-08-91	New York	3B	Lee Guetterman
2569	5-10-91	at Cleveland	2B	Doug Jones
2570	5-13-91	at Cleveland	3B	Charles Nagy
2571	5-13-91	at Cleveland	1B	Bruce Egloff
2572	5-14-91	at New York	2B	John Habyan
2573	5-15-91	at New York	2B	Chuck Cary
2574	5-17-91	at Baltimore	2B	Ben McDonald
2575	5-18-91	at Baltimore	1B	Mike Flanagan

NO.	DATE	OPPONENT	HIT	PITCHER
2576	5-19-91	at Baltimore	1B	Jeff Ballard
2577	5-19-91	at Baltimore	1B	Jeff Ballard
2578	5-20-91	Chicago	HR	Melido Perez
2579	5-21-91	Chicago	1B	Alex Fernandez
2580	5-24-91	Toronto	1B	Duane Ward
2581	5-25-91	Toronto	1B	Todd Stottlemyre
2582	5-26-91	Toronto	2B	David Wells
2583	5-26-91	Toronto	HR	Mike Timlin
2584	5-26-91	Toronto	1B	Willie Fraser
2585	5-28-91	at Chicago	HR	Charlie Hough
2586	5-28-91	at Chicago	2B	Charlie Hough
2587	5-29-91	at Chicago	HR	Greg Hibbard
2588	5-29-91	at Chicago	1B	Greg Hibbard
2589	5-29-91	at Chicago	1B	Melido Perez
2590	5-30-91	at Chicago	1B	Scott Radinsky
2591	5-30-91	at Chicago	1B	Bobby Thigpen
2592	6-01-91	at Toronto	HR	Willie Fraser
2593	6-01-91	at Toronto	1B	Ken Dayley
2594	6-02-91	at Toronto	HR	Jim Acker
2595	6-02-91	at Toronto	1B	Jim Acker
2596	6-05-91	Boston	2B	Mike Gardiner
2597	6-05-91	Boston	2B	Mike Gardiner
2598	6-06-91	Boston	HR	Danny Darwin
2599	6-07-91	Detroit	1B	Frank Tanana
2600	6-07-91	Detroit	1B	Frank Tanana
2601	6-09-91	Detroit	1B	Mike Dalton
2602	6-09-91	Detroit	HR	Mike Dalton
2603	6-10-91	Milwaukee	1B	Chris Bosio
2604	6-10-91	Milwaukee	1B	Chuck Crim
2605	6-12-91	Milwaukee	1B	Ted Higuera
2606	6-14-91	at Boston	3B	Roger Clemens
2607	6-14-91	at Boston	1B	Roger Clemens
2608	6-14-91	at Boston	1B	Roger Clemens
2609	6-17-91	at Boston	1B	Greg A. Harris
2610	6-18-91	at Milwaukee	2B	Ted Higuera
2611	6-18-91	at Milwaukee	HR	Ted Higuera
2612	6-19-91	at Milwaukee	1B	Bill Wegman
2613	6-20-91	at Detroit	1B	Dan Gakeler
2614	6-21-91	at Detroit	1B	Bill Gullickson
2615	6-21-91	at Detroit	1B	Bill Gullickson
2616	6-24-91	at Kansas City	1B	Hector Wagner
2617	6-24-91	at Kansas City	2B	Hector Wagner
2618	6-24-91	at Kansas City	HR	Hector Wagner
2619	6-24-91	at Kansas City	1B	Tom Gordon
2620	6-24-91	at Kansas City	3B	Bill Pecota
2621	6-28-91	Texas	2B	John Barfield
2622	6-28-91	Texas	HR	Calvin Schiraldi
2623	6-29-91	Texas	1B	Gerald Alexander
2624	6-30-91	Texas	HR	Jose Guzman
2625	7-01-91	Texas	HR	Kevin Brown
2626	7-01-91	Texas	1B	Kevin Brown
2627	7-01-91	Texas	1B	Terry Mathews
2628	7-06-91	at Texas	HR	Kevin Brown
2629	7-07-91	at Texas	1B	Nolan Ryan
2630	7-12-91	New York	1B	Scott Kamieniecki
2631	7-14-91	New York	1B	Eric Plunk
2632	7-15-91	Baltimore	1B	Jeff Ballard
2633	7-15-91	Baltimore	1B	Jeff Ballard
2634	7-23-91	at Baltimore	1B	Ben McDonald
2635	7-23-91	at Baltimore	HR	Ben McDonald
2636	7-23-91	at Baltimore	1B	Gregg Olson
2637	7-24-91	at Baltimore	1B	Mike Flanagan
2638	7-25-91	at Baltimore	2B	Mike Flanagan
2639	7-26-91	at New York	1B	Lee Guetterman
2640	7-28-91	at New York	2B	Scott Kamieniecki
2641	7-28-91	at New York	1B	Scott Kamieniecki
2642	7-29-91	at Cleveland	1B	Greg Swindell
2643	7-29-91	at Cleveland	2B	Jeff Shaw
2644	7-29-91	at Cleveland	2B	Rudy Seanez
2645	7-29-91	at Cleveland	1B	Steve Olin
2646	7-31-91	at Detroit	1B	Walt Terrell
2647	7-31-91	at Detroit	1B	Walt Terrell
2648	8-02-91	Seattle	1B	Brian Holman
2649	8-02-91	Seattle	HR	Russ Swan
2650	8-05-91	Minnesota	1B	Kevin Tapani
2651	8-05-91	Minnesota	HR	Kevin Tapani
2652	8-11-91	Oakland	1B	Steve Chitren
2653	8-14-91	at Minnesota	HR	David West
2654	8-16-91	at Seattle	1B	Bill Krueger
2655	8-17-91	at Seattle	1B	Rich DeLucia
2656	8-21-91	at Oakland	1B	Dennis Eckersley
2657	8-23-91	Boston	1B	Matt Young
2658	8-23-91	Boston	1B	Matt Young
2659	8-24-91	Boston	HR	Kevin Morton
2660	8-25-91	Boston	2B	Joe Hesketh

▲ In 1991, Dave led all American League right fielders with a .990 fielding percentage.

▲ Always a fan favorite, Dave poses on Camera Day at Anaheim Stadium.

Joe Carter on Winfield
Joe Carter, Toronto Blue Jays All-Star right fielder who was Dave's Toronto teammate in 1992.

I reflect on what it was like to play with one of the oldest guys to play the game but also one of the greatest guys to play the game. Dave was a guy who you learned a lot from. You see some of the young players these days who come up and they think they know it all; they're not enthused by playing and they don't want to hustle. But last year Dave, at age 40, hustled out every ground ball and took the extra base. It was those little things that you don't notice. He loves the game and he's one of the true professionals. I think of all the people I've played with he's one of the guys I most admire because of his ability and what he did when he went on the field. I can truly say that I had a great time playing with a future Hall of Famer. He's got 3,000 hits and he'll get a lot more after that because he still may be playing when I retire, and that's a compliment to Dave because he keeps himself in shape, he's young at heart and has a great spirit for the game. He's a great person to be around.

Frank Robinson on Winfield
Frank Robinson, Baltimore Orioles Hall of Fame outfielder

Dave Winfield is a player I've always admired from across the field. He always gave all he had on the field and that was guaranteed to be a top performance. He was a feared opponent when he stepped to the plate and when he was on defense because he could beat you either way. For him to get 3,000 hits shows what a steady, consistent player he's been over the course of his career. I'd like to congratulate him on his achievement.

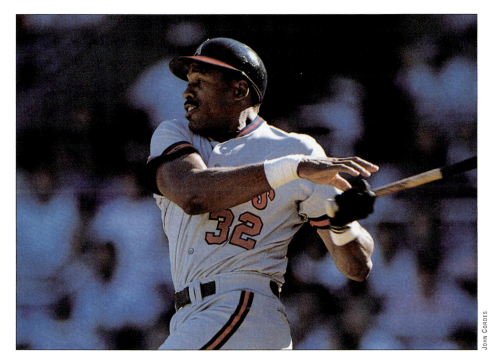

▲ In 1990, Dave led the Angels in RBI, runs and slugging percentage.

NO.	DATE	OPPONENT	HIT	PITCHER
2661	8-25-91	Boston	2B	Dennis Lamp
2662	8-26-91	Detroit	1B	Mark Leiter
2663	8-26-91	Detroit	1B	Mark Leiter
2664	8-27-91	Detroit	1B	John Cerutti
2665	8-27-91	Detroit	1B	John Cerutti
2666	9-02-91	at Milwaukee	2B	Don August
2667	9-03-91	at Boston	1B	Mike Gardiner
2668	9-06-91	Milwaukee	1B	Doug Henry
2669	9-07-91	Milwaukee	1B	Jaime Navarro
2670	9-08-91	Milwaukee	1B	Julio Machado
2671	9-09-91	Texas	HR	Oil Can Boyd
2672	9-09-91	Texas	1B	Terry Mathews
2673	9-11-91	Texas	HR	Brian Bohanon
2674	9-12-91	Chicago	1B	Roberto Hernandez
2675	9-12-91	Chicago	2B	Melido Perez
2676	9-14-91	Chicago	1B	Alex Fernandez
2677	9-14-91	Chicago	1B	Donn Pall
2678	9-17-91	at Texas	1B	Brian Bohanon
2679	9-19-91	at Texas (1)	1B	Nolan Ryan
2680	9-19-91	at Texas (2)	1B	Kevin Brown
2681	9-21-91	at Chicago	1B	Brian Drahman
2682	9-22-91	at Chicago	1B	Greg Hibbard
2683	9-22-91	at Chicago	1B	Greg Hibbard
2684	9-23-91	Toronto	1B	Tom Candiotti
2685	9-26-91	at Kansas City	1B	Mark Gubicza
2686	9-28-91	at Kansas City	1B	Luis Aquino
2687	9-29-91	at Kansas City	HR	Steve Crawford
2688	9-30-91	at Toronto	2B	Jimmy Key
2689	9-30-91	at Toronto	2B	Mike Timlin
2690	10-1-91	at Toronto	1B	Juan Guzman
2691	10-1-91	at Toronto	HR	Jim Acker
2692	10-2-91	at Toronto	1B	Tom Candiotti
2693	10-2-91	at Toronto	HR	David Wells
2694	10-4-91	Kansas City	2B	Luis Aquino
2695	10-4-91	Kansas City	1B	Luis Aquino
2696	10-4-91	Kansas City	1B	Tom Gordon
2697	10-5-91	Kansas City	1B	Kevin Appier

JOHN CORDES

▲ Dave tapes a segment of "On the Ball" with Tommy Lasorda for KMPC Radio in Los Angeles.

started playing ball, when a lot of these people first saw me. This was appropriate."

Winfield finished the 1991 season with impressive numbers for a man who celebrated his 40th birthday at season's end: 28 homers, 86 RBI, 27 doubles, 286 total bases and, defensively, just two errors in right field.

This was on the heels of his 1990 season that earned him American League Comeback Player of the Year honors: 21 homers, 78 RBI and the top field percentage (.988) among everyday right fielders.

Despite Winfield's success over two-plus seasons in Anaheim, the Angels grew weary of the veteran's age and elected to buy out his contract in hopes of using the extra money to sign potential free agents

Bobby Bonilla or Danny Tartabull. "I'll have better numbers than those guys," Winfield said, puzzled and hurt by the Angels' rationale. "I guarantee it."

As it turned out, the Angels failed to land either Bonilla or Tartabull, and eventually offered Winfield a new incentive-laden contract for 1992. However, with his pride stung and all his options open, he decided to sign with the most likely contending team: the Toronto Blue Jays.

And, the next thing the Angels noticed, Winfield was playing for the Blue Jays in the World Series, in which Toronto's victory provided a perfect culmination of that one-year stop on the way home to Minnesota.

Oh, and by the way: He did have better numbers than "those guys." ⚾

Dave rapped career hit number 2,500 on August 7, 1990, versus Boston. ▶

1992

World Series Glory

BY LARRY MILLSON
TORONTO GLOBE AND MAIL

It lasted for such a regrettably short time. One glorious season is all. But for that time, no other player in Blue Jay history has enjoyed the rapport that Dave Winfield had with the Toronto fans.

When he said he'd like to hear the fans make more noise, sure enough the fans became noisy during the drive to a World Series championship and the sign **Winfield Wants Noise** became a SkyDome mainstay.

The crowd sang "Happy Birthday" to him during the second to last game of the season when Winfield turned 41 as the Jays clinched the American League East. Not only had he become a crowd favorite, but he was one of the team's main producers with the bat, hitting 26 home runs with 108 RBI.

It was both fitting and bitterly ironic that it was Winfield who directed the fans to center field at the SkyDome during the 1992 World Series celebrations for the unfurling of the championship banner. No one could have known then that would be Winfield's final act as a Blue Jay. When Paul Molitor was signed as a free agent in December, Winfield was no longer needed and the roar from Toronto fans was startling and prolonged.

Larry Millson is a baseball writer for the Toronto Globe and Mail. Millson covered Dave Winfield and the Toronto Blue Jays during the club's 1992 World Championship season.

The Toronto fans had always liked Winfield in their way even when he was with the hated New York Yankees, long a divisional rival. It had a lot to do with his playing style, of course, but there was also that bizarre incident involving a gull at the old Exhibition Stadium in August of 1983, the year the Jays became a contender for the first time. During a game, one of his warm-up throws between innings hit a gull and killed it. Winfield was charged with cruelty to animals, a charge that was dropped a day later.

The way that Winfield handled the situation made an impression on the Toronto fans. He had a friend, artist Donald Walker, paint a picture with three gulls and a maple leaf with the dedication: "To the Canadian people committed to the preservation of their resources and values." It was auctioned in Toronto at the 1984 Conn Smythe Sports Celebrities Dinner and brought $32,000 for the Easter Seal Society.

Before the Jays signed Winfield as a free agent after the 1991 season, when he was deemed expendable by the California Angels, they had pursued him on the trade market. In 1988, there had almost been a deal with the Yankees that would have

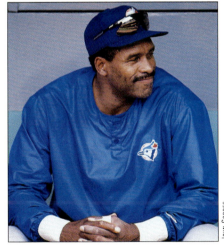

▲ Dave became a Blue Jay in December, 1991.

◄ A very popular Blue Jay, Dave spends time with Toronto fans prior to the 1992 playoffs.

NO.	DATE	OPPONENT	HIT	PITCHER
2698	4-06-92	at Detroit	1B	Bill Gullickson
2699	4-06-92	at Detroit	1B	Bill Gullickson
2700	4-06-92	at Detroit	1B	Bill Gullickson
2701	4-08-92	at Detroit	2B	Frank Tanana
2702	4-09-92	at Detroit	1B	Walt Terrell
2703	4-09-92	at Detroit	HR	Walt Terrell
2704	4-10-92	Baltimore	2B	Mike Mussina
2705	4-11-92	Baltimore	1B	Rick Sutcliffe
2706	4-13-92	New York	1B	Greg Cadaret
2707	4-14-92	New York	1B	Lee Guetterman
2708	4-14-92	New York	1B	Lee Guetterman
2709	4-14-92	New York	HR	Lee Guetterman
2710	4-16-92	New York	1B	Tim Leary
2711	4-16-92	New York	1B	Tim Leary
2712	4-18-92	at Boston	1B	Frank Viola
2713	4-18-92	at Boston	1B	Frank Viola
2714	4-19-92	at Boston	1B	Matt Young
2715	4-20-92	at Boston	1B	Joe Hesketh
2716	4-20-92	at Boston	1B	Greg A. Harris
2717	4-22-92	Cleveland	1B	Charles Nagy
2718	4-22-92	Cleveland	1B	Rod Nichols
2719	4-23-92	Cleveland	1B	Dave Otto
2720	4-23-92	Cleveland	2B	Brad Arnsberg
2721	4-24-92	Kansas City	1B	Tom Gordon
2722	4-25-92	Kansas City	1B	Mike Magnante
2723	4-25-92	Kansas City	1B	Curt Young
2724	4-26-92	Kansas City	1B	Mark Gubicza
2725	4-28-92	California	HR	Chuck Finley
2726	4-28-92	California	HR	Julio Valera
2727	4-29-92	California	1B	Jim Abbott
2728	4-29-92	California	1B	Jim Abbott
2729	4-30-92	at Milwaukee	1B	Chris Bosio
2730	4-30-92	at Milwaukee	1B	Doug Henry
2731	5-01-92	at Milwaukee	2B	Jaime Navarro
2732	5-02-92	at Milwaukee	2B	Dan Plesac
2733	5-03-92	at Milwaukee	HR	Bill Wegman
2734	5-04-92	at Oakland	1B	Ron Darling
2735	5-05-92	at Oakland	2B	Joe Slusarski
2736	5-06-92	at Seattle	2B	Randy Johnson
2737	5-07-92	at Seattle	1B	Erik Hanson
2738	5-07-92	at Seattle	HR	Mike Schooler
2739	5-08-92	at California	1B	Chuck Finley
2740	5-09-92	at California	1B	Jim Abbott
2741	5-13-92	Oakland	3B	Mike Moore
2742	5-15-92	Seattle	1B	Jeff Nelson
2743	5-16-92	Seattle	HR	Clay Parker
2744	5-17-92	Seattle	2B	Randy Johnson
2745	5-18-92	Minnesota	1B	Bill Krueger
2746	5-18-92	Minnesota	1B	Bill Krueger
2747	5-20-92	Minnesota	1B	Scott Erickson
2748	5-23-92	at Chicago	HR	Greg Hibbard
2749	5-29-92	Chicago	1B	Terry Leach
2750	5-31-92	Chicago	1B	Charlie Hough
2751	5-31-92	Chicago	HR	Bobby Thigpen
2752	6-01-92	at Minnesota	2B	Carl Willis
2753	6-02-92	at Minnesota	2B	Pat Mahomes

JOHN CORDES

CHARLES KOCHMAN

Tonya Winfield on Winfield
Tonya Winfield, Dave's wife.

When I was asked to write this testimonial, so many things came to mind that I would want to say about my husband. There are all the wonderful things that he has done for charity through his Foundation and on his own. There are all the great things that he has done in the game of baseball and for the game of baseball. But the most important thing that I can say about him is that he is a gentle giant with a heart to match. I have never known anyone to care about people more than David does. He has a knack for making people feel special. He is a wonderful, loving, caring man and because of that I feel like the luckiest woman in the world to be able to say that he is my husband and best friend.

Paul Molitor on Winfield
Paul Molitor, Toronto Blue Jays All-Star designated hitter and St. Paul native.

Growing up in St. Paul, following in Dave's footsteps, he was rather a legendary figure. When he made the jump from the playgrounds, through high school ball and on to the University of Minnesota, and from there directly to the big leagues, little kids with aspirations of being major leaguers took notice. He paved the way for exposure to many other players in the Twin Cities area. It's been great competing against him at the major league level. He's represented the game with tremendous class and dignity both on and off the field. As he's closed in upon his quest for 3,000 hits, it's been fun to watch a man who's given so much to the game accomplish such a rare milestone. Dave Winfield is a very deserving person.

Jack Morris on Winfield
Jack Morris, Toronto Blue Jays pitcher and St. Paul native who was Dave's Toronto teammate in 1992.

It was a pleasure to play with the guy after growing up in the Twin Cities area and watching him play in front of me both in American Legion ball and collegiate ball. I didn't meet him until I got to the big leagues and I played most of my career against Dave. But it's always a pleasure to be on a team with a guy with Hall of Fame credentials.

▲ Dave played in 156 games for the Blue Jays at the age of 40. Only Pete Rose, Honus Wagner and Darrell Evans played in as many games at the same age.

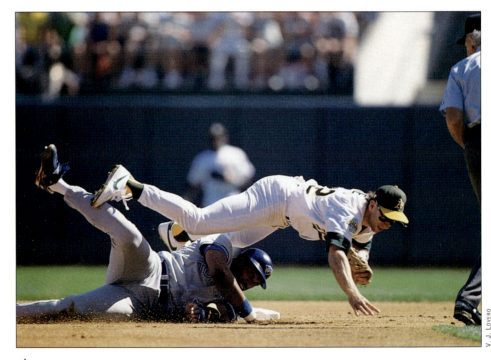

▲ Dave breaks up a double play during the 1992 American League Championship Series versus Oakland.

brought him to Toronto for outfielder Jesse Barfield.

Once he finally was a Jay, Winfield made an impression on the other players and fans immediately. He would go first to third aggressively, stretch singles into doubles, roll into second base to break up double plays and on one play turned a popup into a sacrifice fly. He was 40 and this was only spring training. The message was not lost on younger players and fans alike.

Then there was his tenth career grand slam in the ninth inning that gave the Blue Jays a come-from-behind victory in Seattle on May 7 and the feeling was growing that this could be a special season.

And it turned out that way, of course, thanks to Winfield's 11th-inning double in the sixth game of the World Series that completed the Jays' quest and his own for a first World Series championship.

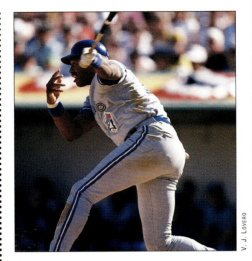

▲ Dave cracked two home runs versus the Athletics in the 1992 American League Championship Series.

V. J. LOVERO

▼ Toronto teammate Pat Tabler has some fun with Dave during the 1992 season.

DAVE WINFIELD 40 YEARS OLD AND STILL THE GREATEST

PHOTO COURTESY OF DAVE AND TONYA WINFIELD

NO.	DATE	OPPONENT	HIT	PITCHER
2754	6-02-92	at Minnesota	1B	Pat Mahomes
2755	6-02-92	at Minnesota	1B	Tom Edens
2756	6-03-92	at Minnesota	1B	Kevin Tapani
2757	6-03-92	at Minnesota	1B	Kevin Tapani
2758	6-03-92	at Minnesota	1B	Kevin Tapani
2759	6-06-92	at Baltimore	2B	Ben McDonald
2760	6-06-92	at Baltimore	2B	Ben McDonald
2761	6-07-92	at Baltimore	2B	Mike Mussina
2762	6-08-92	at New York	2B	Greg Cadaret
2763	6-08-92	at New York	1B	Rich Monteleone
2764	6-10-92	at New York	1B	Shawn Hillegas
2765	6-10-92	at New York	2B	John Habyan
2766	6-11-92	Boston	1B	Roger Clemens
2767	6-11-92	Boston	HR	Roger Clemens
2768	6-13-92	Boston	HR	Joe Hesketh
2769	6-14-92	Boston	1B	Mike Gardiner
2770	6-17-92	Detroit	1B	Walt Terrell
2771	6-18-92	Detroit	1B	Mark Leiter
2772	6-19-92	at Kansas City	1B	Mark Gubicza
2773	6-19-92	at Kansas City	1B	Tom Gordon
2774	6-22-92	at Texas	2B	Terry Mathews
2775	6-22-92	at Texas	HR	Floyd Bannister
2776	6-24-92	at Texas	1B	Bobby Witt
2777	6-26-92	at Cleveland	HR	Jack Armstrong
2778	6-27-92	at Cleveland	1B	Charles Nagy
2779	6-27-92	at Cleveland	2B	Charles Nagy
2780	6-29-92	Texas	1B	Edwin Nunez
2781	6-30-92	Texas	1B	Kevin Brown
2782	6-30-92	Texas	1B	Gerald Alexander
2783	7-03-92	California	1B	Mark Langston
2784	7-03-92	California	1B	Chuck Crim
2785	7-04-92	California	HR	Bert Blyleven
2786	7-05-92	California	1B	Julio Valera
2787	7-06-92	California	1B	Jim Abbott
2788	7-07-92	Seattle	1B	Brian Fisher
2789	7-07-92	Seattle	1B	Brian Fisher
2790	7-08-92	Seattle	2B	Erik Hanson
2791	7-08-92	Seattle	2B	Erik Hanson
2792	7-08-92	Seattle	1B	Erik Hanson
2793	7-16-92	at Seattle	3B	Randy Johnson
2794	7-17-92	at Seattle	2B	Erik Hanson
2795	7-17-92	at Seattle	1B	Juan Agosto
2796	7-18-92	at Seattle	2B	Dave Fleming
2797	7-19-92	at Seattle	2B	Rich DeLucia
2798	7-19-92	at Seattle	HR	Rich DeLucia
2799	7-21-92	at California	2B	Julio Valera
2800	7-22-92	at California	1B	Chuck Finley
2801	7-22-92	at California	HR	Joe Grahe
2802	7-23-92	at Oakland	1B	Mike Moore
2803	7-24-92	at Oakland	1B	Dave Stewart
2804	7-31-92	New York	2B	Tim Leary
2805	8-02-92	New York	3B	Scott Sanderson
2806	8-02-92	New York	1B	Scott Sanderson
2807	8-02-92	New York	2B	John Habyan
2808	8-04-92	at Boston	HR	Greg A. Harris
2809	8-05-92	at Boston	2B	Danny Darwin
2810	8-06-92	at Detroit	HR	Frank Tanana
2811	8-06-92	at Detroit	1B	Mike Munoz
2812	8-07-92	at Detroit	1B	Bill Gullickson
2813	8-07-92	at Detroit	1B	Bill Gullickson
2814	8-07-92	at Detroit	1B	Bill Gullickson
2815	8-08-92	at Detroit	1B	Walt Terrell
2816	8-10-92	Baltimore	2B	Mike Mussina
2817	8-10-92	Baltimore	HR	Mike Mussina
2818	8-12-92	Baltimore	1B	Ben McDonald
2819	8-13-92	Baltimore	1B	Arthur Rhodes
2820	8-14-92	at Cleveland	1B	Rod Nichols
2821	8-16-92	at Cleveland	1B	Dennis Cook
2822	8-16-92	at Cleveland	HR	Dave Otto
2823	8-16-92	at Cleveland	2B	Eric Plunk
2824	8-16-92	at Cleveland	1B	Eric Plunk
2825	8-18-92	at Milwaukee	2B	Bruce Ruffin
2826	8-18-92	at Milwaukee	1B	Doug Henry
2827	8-19-92	at Milwaukee	2B	Chris Bosio
2828	8-20-92	at Milwaukee	1B	Bill Wegman
2829	8-22-92	at Minnesota	1B	Carl Willis
2830	8-26-92	at Chicago	1B	Kirk McCaskill
2831	8-26-92	at Chicago	HR	Bobby Thigpen
2832	8-27-92	Milwaukee	HR	Jaime Navarro
2833	8-27-92	Milwaukee	1B	Darren Holmes
2834	8-28-92	Milwaukee	1B	Cal Eldred
2835	8-29-92	Milwaukee	1B	Doug Henry
2836	8-30-92	Milwaukee	1B	Bill Wegman
2837	8-31-92	Chicago	HR	Terry Leach
2838	9-01-92	Chicago	1B	Donn Pall

NO.	DATE	OPPONENT	HIT	PITCHER
2839	9-02-92	Chicago	1B	Greg Hibbard
2840	9-02-92	Chicago	1B	Greg Hibbard
2841	9-04-92	Minnesota	1B	Tom Edens
2842	9-05-92	Minnesota	1B	John Smiley
2843	9-05-92	Minnesota	1B	Carl Willis
2844	9-06-92	Minnesota	2B	Mike Trombley
2845	9-07-92	at Kansas City	1B	Rick Reed
2846	9-07-92	at Kansas City	1B	Rick Reed
2847	9-07-92	at Kansas City	1B	Jeff Montgomery
2848	9-08-92	at Kansas City	1B	Luis Aquino
2849	9-11-92	at Texas	1B	Scott Chiamparino
2850	9-11-92	at Texas	1B	Roger Pavlik
2851	9-14-92	Cleveland	1B	Jose Mesa
2852	9-15-92	Cleveland	HR	Alan Embree
2853	9-16-92	Cleveland	1B	Charles Nagy
2854	9-17-92	Cleveland	1B	Scott Scudder
2855	9-18-92	Texas	1B	Kevin Brown
2856	9-18-92	Texas	HR	Kevin Brown
2857	9-19-92	Texas	1B	Scott Chiamparino
2858	9-20-92	Texas	1B	Jose Guzman
2859	9-24-92	at Baltimore	HR	Ben McDonald
2860	9-24-92	at Baltimore	2B	Bob Milacki
2861	9-24-92	at Baltimore	1B	Pat Clements
2862	9-27-92	at New York	1B	Scott Sanderson
2863	9-27-92	at New York	1B	Greg Cadaret
2864	9-29-92	Boston	2B	Danny Darwin
2865	10-2-92	Detroit	1B	Walt Terrell
2866	10-2-92	Detroit	1B	Kurt Knudsen

▲ The magic moment: Dave connects for the 1992 World Series-winning double.

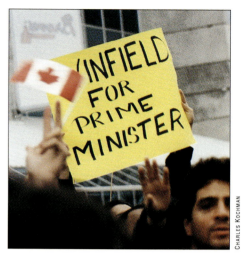

▲ The sign says it all! Fans celebrate Toronto's 1992 world championship.

▲ Dave faces a sea of cameras after Blue Jays win the series.

But the fans knew there was more to the man than baseball and for some of them at least that probably helped give him a special place among the players who have come and gone since the franchise's beginning in 1977. He talked about his travels and his hobbies that include photography. "Baseball is the major part of my life," Winfield said. "It's my job; it's my career. But away from the game, I'm a regular human being. I have other interests, too."

Winfield also expressed an appreciation of what the city of Toronto had to offer. Anyone who explores Toronto's neighborhoods finds out that it has become a city with a multitude of cultures through massive immigration over recent years. Some experts believe Toronto is the most culturally diverse city in the world. This fact is lost on most baseball players, but Winfield said it is something he enjoyed about the city.

"I don't know what other players do," he said, "but I've always explored the city and it's been real cosmopolitan and the people have been nice."

He says he enjoyed the Yorkville area of the city, which is one of the trendier shopping areas that in the '60s was a mecca for the folk clubs but also has a historical aspect to it. But he said he didn't restrict himself to one area.

"I like to mix it up," he said. "I like to see what's up. See the people. Experiment with the food. I'm not locked into one kind of thing. Toronto's up there. The top places in the States are New York, Chicago, San Francisco and Toronto's not far behind."

He might not have been aware of it but there's a faction in Toronto, as there is in many cities, that has an inferiority complex because the city is not New York or Chicago. So the words of a future Hall of Famer saying how much he enjoyed the city had a soothing effect for people who are used to visitors saying something like, "Nice city, so clean."

So when Winfield returned in 1993 with the Minnesota Twins, he received a long ovation from the SkyDome crowd. He was the enemy again but they cheered when he made an out.

But you know he'll always be dear to Toronto fans not only for helping to bring the city a championship, but for the kind of person he is.

Anyone could see that by looking out over the SkyDome crowd on his first night back and reading the signs. There was the obligatory **Winfield Wants Noise**, but there were also banners proclaiming **We Miss You Dave.**

Dave is drenched in champagne following the Blue Jays' 1992 World Series triumph over Atlanta. ▶

Welcome Home, Dave

BY JIM CAPLE
SAINT PAUL PIONEER PRESS

Walk the streets of St. Paul, even the many months when those streets are covered with snow, and you can feel its rich baseball heritage.

That tree there? That's where Paul Molitor fell and broke his first bone. That mound there? That's where Jack Morris once threw a tantrum, hurled a baseball against the backstop and stomped home. That field there? That's where Tim Tschida umped one of his first games and ejected his best friend. And that sandlot there? That's where Peanuts creator Charles Schulz once managed a team and got beat 40-0.

But of all the people to come from this cradle out of baseball, the finest player grew up in a house on Carroll Avenue. The big guy who probably could have excelled in

Jim Caple is the baseball writer for the Saint Paul Pioneer Press. Caple has covered Dave Winfield since he joined the Minnesota Twins prior to the 1993 season.

Kirby Puckett on Winfield
Kirby Puckett, Minnesota Twins All-Star right fielder.

Winnie's one of the classiest guys in the game. After playing against him for nine years, I'm glad I have the opportunity to finally play with him. Some of the things he's achieved in his career, not many players will ever be able to match. He's still playing at the age of 41, is still productive and can drive the ball. He's a great asset to this team because he has brought leadership and a lot of knowledge. He's one of my best friends and I'm glad he came over here. I'm going to be the first guy on the field when he (Winnie) gets 3,000. It's a great accomplishment.

anything he wanted but chose baseball — David Mark Winfield.

The many Gold Gloves and All-Star appearances, the milestone contract and the controversy, the world championship ring and even the dead sea gull — all that came elsewhere for Winfield. But fittingly, the pinnacle of his personal career occurred in a Minnesota uniform. After 20 seasons of major-league ball, Winfield came home for his 3,000th hit.

Unlike Morris in 1991, Winfield shed no tears when he signed with the Twins last December, just flashing that famous grin and pronouncing he wasn't coming home "to just hang around for a few years. I'm going to kick butt."

"I'll see the (younger Twins) running out there with their RBI and home runs," Winfield said before the season, "and I'll say 'Hold, hold, hold on. Here I come.' I'll be right there with them. Or they'll be trying to catch me, probably."

Winfield gave a hint of the excitement to come when he homered in his second at-bat as a Twin and drove in four runs the next night. By the end of the season's first week he had nine RBI. He soon moved past Babe Ruth on the hit chart and became one of the oldest players to ever win the league's player of the week award.

Unfortunately for Minnesota, the next month or so was not productive for either Winfield or the Twins. While Minnesota piled up losing streaks, Winfield's average and production declined as well. By late June he was hitting .234. "Average," he said then to describe his season. "Not average Winfield. Average player." Some, such as

NO.	DATE	OPPONENT	HIT	PITCHER
2867	4-06-93	Chicago	HR	Jack McDowell
2868	4-07-93	Chicago	1B	Kirk McCaskill
2869	4-07-93	Chicago	2B	Scott Radinsky
2870	4-09-93	at Kansas City	2B	Mark Gardner
2871	4-09-93	at Kansas City	HR	Mark Gardner
2872	4-09-93	at Kansas City	2B	Mark Gardner
2873	4-12-93	at Chicago	1B	Kirk McCaskill
2874	4-18-93	Kansas City	1B	Jeff Montgomery
2875	4-20-93	Milwaukee	HR	Jaime Navarro
2876	4-20-93	Milwaukee	1B	Jaime Navarro
2877	4-21-93	Milwaukee	1B	Graeme Lloyd
2878	4-23-93	Detroit	HR	Mike Moore
2879	4-25-93	Detroit	1B	David Wells
2880	4-26-93	at Milwaukee	1B	Ricky Bones
2881	4-26-93	at Milwaukee	1B	Mike Fetters
2882	4-27-93	at Milwaukee	1B	Bill Wegman
2883	4-29-93	at Baltimore	1B	Mike Mussina
2884	5-04-93	Baltimore	1B	Mark Williamson
2885	5-07-93	at Seattle	2B	Dennis Powell
2886	5-08-93	at Seattle	2B	Erik Hanson
2887	5-10-93	at California	1B	John Farrell
2888	5-10-93	at California	1B	John Farrell
2889	5-10-93	at California	1B	Ken Patterson
2890	5-10-93	at California	1B	Chuck Crim
2891	5-11-93	at California	1B	Joe Grahe
2892	5-12-93	at California	HR	Chuck Finley
2893	5-12-93	at California	1B	Chuck Finley
2894	5-15-93	Boston	1B	John Dopson
2895	5-15-93	Boston	HR	John Dopson
2896	5-15-93	Boston	HR	Scott Bankhead
2897	5-16-93	Boston	1B	Paul Quantrill
2898	5-16-93	Boston	2B	Joe Hesketh
2899	5-17-93	New York	1B	Jimmy Key
2900	5-17-93	New York	2B	Jimmy Key
2901	5-17-93	New York	1B	John Habyan
2902	5-19-93	New York	2B	Bob Wickman
2903	5-25-93	at Oakland	1B	Storm Davis
2904	5-28-93	Cleveland	1B	Mark Clark
2905	5-29-93	Cleveland	1B	Mike Bielecki
2906	5-29-93	Cleveland	1B	Mike Bielecki
2907	5-31-93	Texas	1B	Charlie Leibrandt
2908	6-06-93	at Cleveland	1B	Dennis Cook
2909	6-08-93	at Texas	3B	Todd Burns
2910	6-08-93	at Texas	1B	Matt Whiteside
2911	6-10-93	at Texas	1B	Charlie Leibrandt
2912	6-12-93	Oakland	1B	Bobby Witt
2913	6-13-93	Oakland	1B	Shawn Hillegas
2914	6-14-93	Toronto	1B	Danny Cox
2915	6-17-93	at New York	1B	Mike Witt
2916	6-17-93	at New York	1B	John Habyan
2917	6-18-93	at New York	1B	Jimmy Key
2918	6-18-93	at New York	1B	Bobby Munoz
2919	6-19-93	at New York	1B	Scott Kamieniecki
2920	6-21-93	at Boston	1B	John Dopson
2921	6-23-93	at Boston	1B	Aaron Sele
2922	6-29-93	Seattle	1B	Tim Leary

◀ The hit: Dave becomes a member of the 3,000 hit club.

Robin Yount on Winfield
Robin Yount, Milwaukee Brewers outfielder who is a member of the 3,000 hit club.

Dave Winfield is a hard-nosed type player who goes out there with one thing in mind, and that's to beat the other guy. He's been a dominant offensive player. With the type of offense he can produce he's a player who can almost single-handedly carry a team when it's struggling. He's an offensive player that everyone would love to have on their team. I'm sure that getting 3,000 is a real thrill for Dave. He's played a long time. He seemed pretty excited about the fact that he had a good opportunity to get 3,000 hits. I think, without a doubt, that it will be something that he'll always remember.

George Brett on Winfield
George Brett, Kansas City Royals designated hitter who is a member of the 3,000 hit club.

Dave Winfield is one of the most feared hitters in the game. Feared not only for a base hit but the fear of the long ball. He is a good RBI man and clutch hitter. He is a player to look up to for what he has done on and off the field.

Cal Ripken, Jr., on Winfield
Cal Ripken, Jr., Baltimore Orioles All-Star shortstop.

When I think of Dave Winfield, I think of a very good hitter and a very good RBI man. But, it's his extra-base power that really stands out. Not only does he hit home runs, but the balls jump off his bat into both gaps and off both fences. He can drive the ball to any part of the field and he makes outfielders misjudge his balls because he hits them so hard with backspin. He's been so consistent; he's a great all-around player. He runs the bases hard and can steal a base when he needs to. In my opinion, the ball jumps off his bat harder than any other player in the league. To me, 3,000 hits signifies he's done a good job for a long time. In order to get 3,000 hits, you have to be consistent for a very long time. When I think about the people who have done it, like Robin Yount and George Brett, and now Dave Winfield, I think about people who keep putting up strong numbers every year.

▲ Owner Carl Pohlad welcomes Dave to the Twins' organization, Dec. 18, 1992.

▲ Dave takes a break at spring training.

manager Tom Kelly, said Winfield was feeling the pressure of 3,000 hits. Some doubted he would reach 3,000 this season. Others speculated age was beginning to catch up even to him.

Winfield, of course, expressed no such doubts. He had weathered many slumps in his long career and knew this one would end, too. And it did. After a long study of a high-light tape ,"My greatest hits collection," he called it, Winfield broke out of the slump with two hits June 29 and a home run the next night. A couple of nights later, there was a four-hit game. "I'm tired of lounging in unfamiliar territory," he said. "I'm not used to being in the .230s, .240s and .250s." The rush toward 3,000 was on.

He averaged almost two hits a game for a long stretch. One night he hit a home run off the team bus. Another day he hit a home run after a pre-game old-timers contest featuring several players younger than Winfield. A couple of weeks later, another old-timers game, another home run —Winfield's 450th.

Before long, he found himself in a familiar territory leading his club in home runs and RBI, near the top in average.

As he raced down the path toward 3,000, he also was fitting in more and more with his new teammates, some of them two

Dave reacts to an umpire's call during a ▶ Twins home game in May.

Rod Carew on Winfield
Rod Carew, a member of the Hall of Fame, current California Angels' hitting coach, former Twins' great and a member of the 3,000 hit club.

Dave Winfield was destined to be a star years ago. Fortunately, he chose baseball as his stage. His accomplishments with San Diego, the Yankees, California, Toronto and now Minnesota have been well chronicled. It was satisfying seeing Dave achieve his ultimate goal last season as a member of the Blue Jays when he was part of a World Championship team. But last year was a team accomplishment; 3,000 hits is a personal accomplishment. When I started my career with Minnesota, reaching 3,000 hits was not something I considered. However, once there, it was an honor to look at the baseball greats who had already done so. Though Dave has been recognized for his power and run production, reaching 3,000 hits symbolizes something he's probably most satisfied with: consistency. Welcome to the 3,000 hit club, Dave, your arrival has been long anticipated.

▲ Dave and fellow Minnesota native Kent Hrbek
work out at spring training.

▲ Dave watches the flight of the ball against the Orioles
at the Metrodome.

◀ Twins manager, Tom Kelly, talks strategy with Dave.

NO.	DATE	OPPONENT	HIT	PITCHER
2923	6-29-93	Seattle	1B	Mike Hampton
2924	6-30-93	Seattle	HR	Randy Johnson
2925	6-30-93	Seattle	1B	Norm Charlton
2926	7-02-93	Milwaukee	1B	Cal Eldred
2927	7-02-93	Milwaukee	HR	Mike Ignasiak
2928	7-03-93	Milwaukee	1B	Ricky Bones
2929	7-04-93	Milwaukee	1B	Jaime Navarro
2930	7-04-93	Milwaukee	1B	Jaime Navarro
2931	7-04-93	Milwaukee	HR	Jaime Navarro
2932	7-05-93	Detroit	HR	David Wells
2933	7-05-93	Detroit	1B	Tom Bolton
2934	7-06-93	Detroit	2B	John Doherty
2935	7-07-93	Detroit	2B	Bill Gullickson
2936	7-08-93	at Milwaukee	1B	Ricky Bones
2937	7-08-93	at Milwaukee	1B	Ricky Bones
2938	7-09-93	at Milwaukee	1B	Jaime Navarro
2939	7-09-93	at Milwaukee	2B	Jaime Navarro
2940	7-09-93	at Milwaukee	HR	Matt Maysey
2941	7-09-93	at Milwaukee	1B	Graeme Lloyd
2942	7-10-93	at Milwaukee	1B	James Austin
2943	7-10-93	at Milwaukee	HR	Doug Henry
2944	7-15-93	at Baltimore	2B	Ben McDonald
2945	7-16-93	at Baltimore	HR	Mike Mussina
2946	7-16-93	at Baltimore	2B	Todd Frohwirth
2947	7-18-93	at Baltimore	1B	Fernando Valenzuela
2948	7-19-93	at Detroit	1B	Sean Bergman
2949	7-19-93	at Detroit	1B	Sean Bergman
2950	7-20-93	at Detroit	1B	Mike Moore
2951	7-21-93	at Detroit	1B	David Wells
2952	7-21-93	at Detroit	2B	Kurt Knudsen
2953	7-22-93	Baltimore	2B	Rick Sutcliffe
2954	7-24-93	Baltimore	3B	Jamie Moyer
2955	7-24-93	Baltimore	2B	Jamie Moyer
2956	7-25-93	Baltimore	1B	Ben McDonald
2957	7-25-93	Baltimore	HR	Todd Frohwirth
2958	7-27-93	at Seattle	HR	Chris Bosio
2959	7-27-93	at Seattle	1B	Chris Bosio
2960	7-28-93	at Seattle	HR	Randy Johnson
2961	7-28-93	at Seattle	1B	Brad Holman
2962	7-29-93	at Seattle	1B	Ted Power
2963	7-31-93	at California	2B	Chuck Finley
2964	8-01-93	at California	HR	Russ Springer
2965	8-01-93	at California	1B	Gene Nelson
2966	8-03-93	Boston	1B	John Dopson
2967	8-03-93	Boston	1B	Greg A. Harris
2968	8-04-93	Boston	2B	Aaron Sele
2969	8-04-93	Boston	1B	Aaron Sele
2970	8-04-93	Boston	1B	Paul Quantrill
2971	8-06-93	New York	1B	Bob Wickman
2972	8-07-93	New York	1B	Jim Abbott
2973	8-07-93	New York	1B	Jim Abbott
2974	8-07-93	New York	1B	Jim Abbott
2975	8-10-93	at Toronto	1B	Dave Stewart
2976	8-12-93	at Toronto	1B	Jack Morris
2977	8-13-93	at Oakland	1B	Ron Darling
2978	8-13-93	at Oakland	1B	Ron Darling
2979	8-14-93	at Oakland (1)	1B	Bobby Witt
2980	8-14-93	at Oakland (1)	1B	Edwin Nunez
2981	8-17-93	Kansas City	1B	Chris Haney
2982	8-20-93	Chicago	1B	Alex Fernandez
2983	8-22-93	Chicago	1B	Jack McDowell
2984	8-23-93	at Kansas City	1B	Kevin Appier
2985	8-26-93	at Chicago	1B	Mike Magnante
2986	8-27-93	at Chicago (1)	2B	Tim Belcher
2987	8-27-93	at Chicago (2)	HR	Jack McDowell
2988	8-27-93	at Chicago (2)	1B	Donn Pall
2989	8-29-93	at Chicago	1B	Kirk McCaskill
2990	8-31-93	Cleveland	2B	Jeff Mutis
2991	9-02-93	Cleveland	2B	Jerry DiPoto
2992	9-03-93	Texas	HR	Rick Reed
2993	9-08-93	at Cleveland	1B	Jose Mesa
2994	9-08-93	at Cleveland	1B	Jose Mesa
2995	9-09-93	at Cleveland	2B	Eric Plunk
2996	9-09-93	at Cleveland	1B	Jerry DiPoto
2997	9-13-93	Oakland	HR	Bobby Witt
2998	9-15-93	Oakland	1B	Todd Van Poppel
2999	9-16-93	Oakland	1B	Kelly Downs
3000	9-16-93	Oakland	1B	Dennis Eckersley

Devon White on Winfield
Devon White, Toronto Blue Jays All-Star center fielder who was Dave's Toronto teammate in 1992.

I enjoyed playing with Dave, first in California, then in Toronto. He's a motivator, knows the game well and works well with the young players. He helped me to get mentally and physically prepared for each at-bat, each game, each situation, how to handle the press, etc. He is someone that I looked up to as a big brother. I consider him a good friend.

Cito Gaston on Winfield
Cito Gaston, Toronto Blue Jays manager and Dave's San Diego teammate from 1973-74.

I'm probably one of the guys who has known Dave Winfield ever since he first began playing professional baseball. One thing you knew about Dave right away was the he was going to be a good player and he had all the desire in the world to make himself better. Dave Winfield has always been his own man and is a winner. He's a Hall of Famer as far as I'm concerned. It was a pleasure, an honor and a thrill to have him on our ballclub in 1992 because he did so much for us as far as leadership both on and off the field. Whatever Dave does after baseball I'm sure he's going to be just as successful as when he played.

Tom Seaver on Winfield
Tom Seaver, member of the Baseball Hall of Fame who won 311 games in his 20 year career.

David Winfield was one of the most aggressive hitters I ever faced. He had tremendous power, and I would say that he would be in the top five on my list of players that I faced in my career who could take advantage of a pitcher's mistake. If you made a mistake to him he may not have hit the ball out of the ballpark, but he was absolutely the one individual who was going to crush it. Dave was a great competitor, a great defensive player, a great baserunner and is headed for the Hall of Fame.

▲ The aggressive swing that has led to 3,000 hits.

▲ Dave acknowledges the Metrodome crowd after his first home run as a Twin on opening night, April 6, 1993.

decades younger. It was a little difficult at first, but by mid-season, he was often entertaining them with tales of the old days.

"The Padres had their own plane," he said one day. "It was a prop plane ... I'm serious. We had one coach in charge of bringing us drinks. Really."

"It's great having him here," Kirby Puckett said. "He's always instigating. He's like having another Puck around. And he's achieving something, too."

Achieving, indeed. Three thousand hits. Welcome home, David.

"It's a good time for me in life. It really is," Winfield said. "I understand what I'm doing. I don't worry about what I'm doing. I can just say it's a pretty good time and it's good to be back home again."

TOPPS BASEBALL CARDS

1974 • 1993

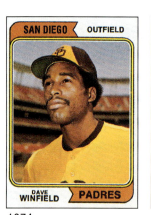
1974

1975

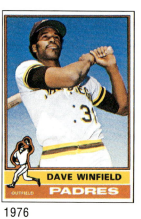
1976

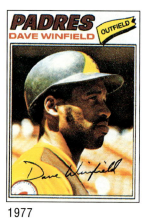
1977

1978

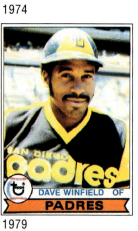
1979

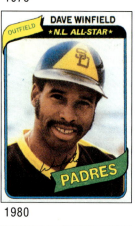
1980

1981

1982

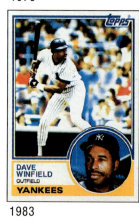
1983

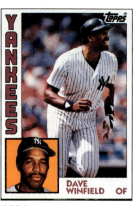
1984

1985

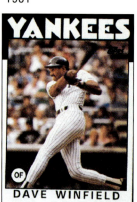
1986

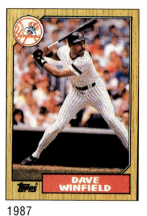
1987

1988

1989

1990

1991

1992

1993

DAVE WINFIELD
TWINS

CAP ANSON

Born: April 11, 1852, at Marshalltown, IA
Died: April 14, 1922, at Chicago, IL
Elected to Hall of Fame in 1939

Playing Career: Rockford Forest Citys (NA) 1871 / Philadelphia Athletics (NA) 1872-75 / Chicago Cubs (NL) 1876-97

Manager: Chicago Cubs (NL) 1879-97 / New York Giants (NL) 1898

Known as "Pop"... First player to collect 3,000 hits ... He also was the oldest (46 years, 2 months, 7 days) to attain it ... Accomplished the feat on July 18, 1897 ... It was a fourth inning single ... The feat never made the Chicago newspapers ... Anson was the foremost on-field baseball figure of the 19th century ... Led the National League in hitting three times (1879, 1881 and 1888) ... Was the first to hit .400 twice (.407 in 1879 and .421 in 1887)

Playing Career	AVG.	G	AB	R	H	2B	3B	HR	RBI	BB	SO	SB
22 Years	.329	2276	9108	1719	3041	528	124	96	1715	952	294	247

HONUS WAGNER

Born: February 24, 1874, at Mansfield, PA
Died: December 6, 1955, at Carnegie, PA
Elected to Hall of Fame in 1936

Playing Career: Louisville (NL) 1897-1899
Pittsburgh Pirates (NL) 1900-17

Manager: Pittsburgh Pirates (NL) 1917

Known as the "Flying Dutchman" ... Considered the greatest all-around player ... Played every position except catcher ... Broke into the major leagues with a .338 batting average in 1897 and produced 17 .300-plus seasons, including eight National League batting titles ... Was the first player to have his signature on a Louisville Slugger baseball bat (1905) ... His 1909 baseball card is worth over $100,000 ... A flawless fielder, he was a brilliant base runner, amassing 720 stolen bases, topping the league in thefts six times ... Collected his 3,000th hit, a double, on June 9, 1914 ... Was one of the original five players (Ty Cobb, Babe Ruth, Christy Mathewson and Walter Johnson) elected to the Hall of Fame.

Playing Career	AVG.	G	A	B	R	H	2B	HR	RBI	BB	SO	SB
21 Years	.327	2789	10,441	1735	3418	643	252	101	1732	963	327	722

NAP LAJOIE

Born: September 5, 1874, at Woonsocket, RI
Died: February 7, 1959, at Daytona Beach, FL
Elected to Hall of Fame in 1937

Playing Career: Philadelphia Phillies (NL) 1896-1901
Philadelphia Athletics (AL) 1901-02; 1915-16
Cleveland Indians (AL) 1902-14

Manager: Cleveland Indians (AL) 1905-09

Considered the greatest second baseman to ever play the game ... Topped the .300 mark 16 times, including 10 times over .350 ... Won three batting crowns during his day, including .422 in his first American League campaign ... During the dead-ball era, was known as a powerful pull-hitter, collecting 893 extra-base hits ... On September 15, 1914, became the first American League player to reach the 3,000 hit plateau ... A fan favorite, he was a player-manager for five seasons and the club was called the "Naps" in his honor ... Was the sixth player elected to the Hall of Fame.

Playing Career	AVG.	G	A	B	R	2B	3B	HR	RBI	BB	SO	SB
21 Years	.338	2479	9592	1503	3244	658	161	83	1599	516	85	382

◀ The Metrodome crowd is on its feet as Dave Winfield follows through on the swing that netted him his 3,000th hit.

TY COBB

Born: December 18, 1886, at Narrows, GA
Died: July 17, 1961, at Atlanta, GA
Elected to Hall of Fame in 1936

Playing Career: Detroit Tigers (AL) 1905-26
Philadelphia Athletics (AL) 1927-28

Manager: Detroit Tigers (AL) 1921-26

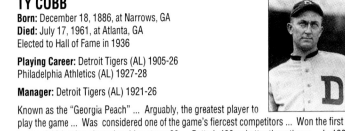

Known as the "Georgia Peach" ... Arguably, the greatest player to play the game ... Was considered one of the game's fiercest competitors ... Won the first of a record 12 batting championships at age 20 ... Batted .400 or better three times ... In 1909, he was the first player to win the Triple Crown ... In 1911, set the American League record when he hit safely in 41 consecutive games, now the fourth longest batting streak in modern-day history ... Also was named the Most Valuable Player in 1911 ... Is the youngest player (34 years, 8 months, 1 day) to reach the 3,000 hit level, accomplishing the feat on August 19, 1921 ... His lifetime .367 batting average is a major-league record ... As one of the original five players inducted to Baseball's Hall of Fame, he was the top vote-getter, receiving 222 of a possible 226 ballots, seven more than Babe Ruth and Honus Wagner.

Playing Career	AVG.	G	AB	R	H	2B	3B	HR	RBI	BB	SO	SB
24 Years	.367	3034	11,429	2245	4191	724	297	118	1961	1249	357	892

TRIS SPEAKER

Born: April 4, 1888, at Hubbard, TX
Died: December 8, 1958, at Lake Whitney, TX
Elected to Hall of Fame in 1937

Playing Career:
Boston Red Sox (AL) 1907-15 / Cleveland Indians (AL) 1916-26
Washington Senators (AL) 1927 / Philadelphia Athletics (AL) 1928

Manager: Cleveland Indians (AL) 1919-26

Known as the "Gray Eagle" ... Revolutionized outfield play by positioning himself in shallow center field ... As a rookie, Cy Young would hit him fly balls to sharpen his ability ... Holds the major-league record with 448 assists from the outfield ... On his Hall of Fame plaque there is an inscription that reads "greatest center fielder of his day" ... Incredibly won only one batting title during his career, despite a .344 lifetime average ... He is the all-time leader with 793 career doubles, leading the American League eight times in that category ... In 1912, he won the AL home run title and the Chalmers AL award (predecessor of the MVP) ... He also ranks fifth in hits, seventh in triples and eighth in runs scored ... Collected his 3,000th career hit on May 17, 1925 .

Playing Career	AVG.	G	AB	R	H	2B	3B	HR	RBI	BB	SO	SB
22 Years	.344	2789	10,208	1881	3515	792	223	117	1559	1381	220	433

EDDIE COLLINS

Born: May 2, 1887, at Millerton, NY
Died: March 25, 1951, at Boston, MA
Elected to Hall of Fame in 1939

Playing Career: Philadelphia Athletics (AL) 1906-14
Chicago White Sox (AL) 1915-26 / Philadelphia Athletics (AL) 1927-30

Manager: Chicago White Sox (AL) 1925-26

Known as "Cocky" ... An aggressive and confident second baseman, he was known for his outstanding ability to steal bases ... Holds the American League record with 25 years of service ... Although he never won a batting title he batted better than .340 on 10 occasions ... He was one of the first players to use a choke grip batting style ... Topped the American League four times in stolen bases and nine times led all second baseman in fielding ... Played on six World Series teams, including the infamous 1919 Chicago "Black Sox" ... Not involved in the scandal, he was unforgiving of his eight teammates who were found guilty of "fixing" the series against the Cincinnati Reds ... On June 6, 1925, he doubled off Detroit's Walter Johnson for his 3,000th career hit.

Playing Career	AVG.	G	AB	R	H	2B	3B	HR	RBI	BB	SO	SB
25 Years	.333	2826	9949	1818	3311	437	187	47	1299	1503	286	743

PAUL WANER

Born: April 16, 1903, at Harrah, OK
Died: August 29, 1965, at Sarasota, FL
Elected to Hall of Fame in 1952

Playing Career: Pittsburgh Pirates (NL) 1926-40 / Brooklyn Dodgers (NL) 1941; 1943-44 / Boston Braves (NL) 1941-42 New York Yankees (AL) 1944-45

Known as "Big Poison" ... Older brother of Lloyd "Little Poison," who was elected to the Hall of Fame in 1967 ... Paul was a speedy outfielder with a rifle throwing arm, perhaps possessing the strongest throwing arm seen in Pittsburgh until Roberto Clemente ... A line drive hitter, who won three National League batting titles while topping the .300 plateau 14 times during his career ... In 1927, he led the Pirates to the NL pennant by batting .380 with 237 hits,17 triples and 131 RBI, earning his only National League Most Valuable Player award.

Playing Career	AVG	G	AB	R	H	2B	3B	HR	RBI	BB	SO	SB
20 Years	.333	2549	9459	1626	3152	603	190	112	1309	1091	376	104

STAN MUSIAL

Born: November 21, 1920, at Donora, PA
Elected to Hall of Fame in 1969

Playing Career: St. Louis Cardinals (NL) 1941-63

Known as "Stan the Man" ... The first genuine power-hitter to surpass the 3,000 hit level ... He accomplished the feat on May 13, 1958 ... Noted for his compressed, closed stance ... One of the more consistent hitters to play the game, he had 1,815 hits at home and 1,815 hits on the road ... He scored 1,949 runs and drove in another 1,951 runs ... He amassed 1,377 extra-base hits, ranking among the majors, all-time leaders in double, triples and home runs ... A three-time National League Most Valuable Player, he is one of only three players (other two are Detroit's Hank Greenberg and Milwaukee Brewers Robin Yount) to ever earn the distinction at two different positions ... Batted better than .300 18 times during his career, leading the NL in batting seven times, including in three consecutive seasons.

Playing Career	AVG	G	AB	R	H	2B	3B	HR	RBI	BB	SO	SB
22 Years	.331	3026	10972	1949	3630	725	177	475	1951	1599	696	78

HENRY AARON

Born: February 5, 1934, at Mobile, AL
Elected to Hall of Fame in 1982

Playing Career: Milwaukee Braves (NL) 1954-65
Atlanta Braves (NL) 1966-74 / Milwaukee Brewers (AL) 1975-76

Known as "Hammerin' Hank" ... The all-time home run king with 755 homers ... On April 8, 1974, he entered the record book with his 715th home run, surpassing Babe Ruth ... He accomplished the feat off Los Angeles' Al Downing in Atlanta ... Aaron also set all-time records in total bases, extra-base hits and runs batted in; second in at-bats and runs scored and third in games played ... Hit 40 or more home runs on eight occasions while driving in 100 or more runs a dozen times in a season ... Is the second youngest player (36 years, 4 months, 12 days) to collect his 3,000th career hit, that coming on May 17, 1970 ... By doing so, he was the first to reach that plateau in 12 years ... He led the National League in batting twice, home runs and RBI four times ... Was named The Sporting News "Player of the Year" in 1956 and 1963 ... Three-time Gold Glove outfielder ... In 1957, he led the Milwaukee Braves to their only World Championship, earning the NL's Most Valuable Player award.

Playing Career	AVG	G	AB	R	H	2B	3B	HR	RBI	BB	SO	SB
23 Years	.305	3298	12,364	2174	3771	624	98	755	2297	1402	1383	240

WILLIE MAYS

Born: May 6, 1931, at Westfield, AL
Elected to Hall of Fame in 1979

Playing Career: New York Giants (NL) 1951-57
San Francisco Giants (NL) 1958-72 / New York Mets (NL) 1972-73

Known as "The Say Hey Kid" ... Judged as perhaps the greatest player of all time ... A paradigm of the complete player; he could hit for power and average, steal bases, play the field and throw the baseball ... Along with Henry Aaron and Mickey Mantle, Mays was one of the top sluggers in the game during the 1950s and 1960s ... An electrifying talent, he was named the 1951 National League Rookie of the Year ... His totals rank on baseball's all-time list, including third in homers, fifth in runs scored and seventh in RBI ... A two-time Most Valuable Player, he led the National League in home runs four times ... Ironically, he won just one batting title, that coming in 1954, despite hitting over .300 10 times during his career ... He managed to hit 51 homers in 1955 and 52 homers in 1965, becoming one of only five players (Babe Ruth, Jimmie Foxx, Ralph Kiner and Mickey Mantle) to hit 50 or more homers more than once ... He earned his 3,000th career hit on July 18, 1970.

Playing Career	AVG	G	AB	R	H	2B	3B	HR	RBI	BB	SO	SB
22 Years	.302	2992	10,881	2062	3283	523	140	660	1903	1463	1526	338

ROBERTO CLEMENTE

Born: August 18, 1934, at Carolina, PR
Died: December 31, 1972, at San Juan, PR
Elected to Hall of Fame in 1973

Playing Career: Pittsburgh Pirates (NL) 1955-72

Admired for his intensity for the game ... Spectacular defensive talent, noted for having a strong throwing arm, exceptional range and an uncanny ability to make leaping and diving catches ... Won 12 consecutive Gold Gloves as a right fielder and set a major-league record by leading the National League in assists five times ... Offensively, batted better than .300 13 times during his career, including eight straight seasons in which he hit over .312 ... Batted over .340 five times ... Won four batting titles, batting .351 in 1961 and a career high .357 in 1967 ... Was named the National League Most Valuable Player in 1966 ... He was named to the NL All-Star team 12 times during his career ... On September 30, 1972, a fourth inning double off New York Mets' Jon Matlack at Three Rivers Stadium marked his 3,000th hit — it also would be his last ... On New Year's Eve of 1972, Clemente died in a plane crash while flying relief supplies to Nicaraguan earthquake victims ... The mandatory five-year waiting period for Hall of Fame induction was waived for Clemente, who was elected in 1973.

Playing Career	AVG	G	AB	R	H	2B	3B	HR	RBI	BB	SO	SB
18 Years	.317	2433	9454	1416	3000	440	166	240	1305	621	1230	83

AL KALINE

Born: December 19, 1934, at Baltimore, MD
Elected to Hall of Fame in 1980

Playing Career: Detroit Tigers (AL) 1953-74

Known as "Mr. Tiger" ... A model of consistency ... Ranks among Detroit's all-time leaders in virtually every offensive category, including topping the list in games played and home runs ... Joined the Tigers at the tender age of 18 ... Became the second youngest player to ever hit a grand slam home run ... Batted over .300 nine times in his career ... Won just one batting title, that coming in 1955 when he hit a career best .340 ... At age 20, he was the youngest player to ever win a batting crown ... It also was the only season he collected 200 hits ... Finished second to Yogi Berra in the American League Most Valuable Player balloting ... He reached the 3,000 hit plateau on September 24, 1974 ... After retiring, he moved to the Tigers broadcast booth.

Playing Career	AVG	G	AB	R	H	2B	3B	HR	RBI	BB	SO	SB
22 Years	.297	2834	10,116	1622	3007	498	75	399	1583	1277	1020	137

PETE ROSE

Born: April 14, 1941, at Cincinnati, OH

Playing Career: Cincinnati Reds (NL) 1963-78; 1985-86 Philadelphia Phillies (NL) 1979-84 / Montreal Expos (NL) 1984

Manager: Cincinnati Reds (NL) 1984-89

Known as "Charlie Hustle" ... A player's player ... No one played the game with the same fervor that he did ... Unquestionably, the greatest switch-hitter ever ... Two of his trademarks were his headfirst slides and sprinting to first base when issued a base-on-balls ... Played in more seasons than any other National League player ... In his later years, was noted for bouncing the baseball on the artificial turf when recording the final put-out of an inning ... The all-time hit leader, surpassing Ty Cobb record many felt would never be broken ... He established the all-time hit record on September 11, 1985, when he singled off San Diego's Eric Show at Riverfront Stadium ... Also holds the all-time marks in singles, games played and at-bats while he is runner-up in doubles and fourth in runs scored ... One of the youngest players (37 years, 0 months, 21 days) to reach the 3,000 hit class ... He accomplished that feat on May 5, 1978 ... That same season, set the National League modern-day record with a 44-game hitting streak, second in baseball history to Joe DiMaggio's legendary 56-game streak set in 1941 ... Named The Sporting News "Player of the Decade" for the 1970s ... Won a pair of Gold Gloves.

Playing Career	AVG	G	AB	R	H	2B	3B	HR	RBI	BB	SO	SB
24 Years	.303	3562	14,053	2165	4256	746	135	160	1314	1566	1143	198

LOU BROCK

Born: June 18, 1939, at El Dorado, AR
Elected to Hall of Fame in 1985

Playing Career: Chicago Cubs (NL) 1961-64 St. Louis Cardinals (NL) 1964-79

The greatest base stealer in National League history ... Holds the NL record with 938 career steals and 118 in a season (1974) ... Rickey Henderson holds the major-league marks, surpassing the 1,000 career total this season and establishing the single season standard of 130 in 1982 ... Although famous for his speed, Brock did have some power, hitting a 500-foot home run at the old Polo Grounds on June 17, 1962 ... Four times during his career he amassed 200 hits ... Twice he led the league in runs scored while also finding himself atop of the leader board in doubles and triples ... A four-time All-Star, he led the St. Louis Cardinals to three National League pennants and the 1964 and 1967 World Championships ... Before retiring following the 1979 season, he became the last National League player to attain 3,000 career hits ... Brock accomplished the feat on August 13, 1979, against the Chicago Cubs, the only other team he ever played for.

Playing Career	AVG	G	AB	R	H	2B	3B	HR	RBI	BB	SO	SB
19 Years	.293	2616	10,332	1610	3023	486	141	149	900	761	1730	938

CARL YASTRZEMSKI

Born: August 22, 1939, at Southampton, NY
Elected to Hall of Fame in 1989

Playing Career: Boston Red Sox (AL) 1961-83

Known as "Yaz" ... Replaced the legendary Ted Williams in left field, then followed him to Cooperstown ... Boston's all-time leader in games played, at-bats, runs, hits, doubles, total bases, runs batted in and extra-base hits ... Yaz played with graceful intensity in more games than any other American League player ... Despite hitting over .300 just six times during his career, he managed to win three batting titles ... One of only 11 players to ever win the Triple Crown ... He is the last one to accomplish the "Hat Trick," batting .326 with 44 home runs and 121 RBI in 1967, the only season he was named the American League Most Valuable Player ... On September 12, 1979, Yaz singled against the New York Yankees for his 3,000th career hit ... He was one of five to reach that plateau at the age of 40 or more.

Playing Career	AVG	G	AB	R	H	2B	3B	HR	RBI	BB	SO	SB
23 Years	285	3308	11,988	1816	3419	646	59	452	1844	1845	1393	168

ROD CAREW

Born: October 1, 1945, at Gaton, Panama
Elected to Hall of Fame in 1991

Playing Career: Minnesota Twins (AL) 1967-78 California Angels (AL) 1979-85

A wizard with the bat, he lined, chopped and bunted his way to becoming the first player in nearly six seasons to reach the 3,000 hit plateau ... He accomplished the feat on August 4, 1985 ... Was named the American League Rookie of the Year in 1967 and 10 years later, earned his only AL Most Valuable Player honor after setting career highs with a .388 average, 239 hits, 16 triples and 128 runs scored ... His seven batting titles — four consecutive — are surpassed only by Ty Cobb and Honus Wagner ... He hit over .300 in 15 consecutive seasons from 1969-83 and missed the mark in two other seasons by less than 10 percentage points.

Playing Career	AVG	G	AB	R	H	2B	3B	HR	RBI	BB	SO	SB
19 Years	.328	2469	9315	1424	3053	445	112	92	1015	1018	1028	353

ROBIN YOUNT

Born: September 16, 1955, at Danville, IL

Playing Career: Milwaukee Brewers (AL) 1974-Present

One of the greatest all-around players in American League history ... The Milwaukee Brewers all-time leader in nearly every offensive category ... He broke into the game as a shortstop, winning a Gold Glove in 1982 ... Also earned AL Most Valuable Player award in 1982 when he led the league with 210 hits ... A three-time All-Star, he batted .414 in his lone World Series appearance for Milwaukee versus St. Louis in 1982 ... Earned his second AL Most Valuable Player award as a center fielder in 1989, making him the third player in history to win MVP honors at two different positions ... Named USA TODAY AL Player of the Decade for the 1980s ... Became the 17th player in major-league history to record 3,000 career hits September 9, 1992, versus Cleveland.

Playing Career	AVG	G	AB	R	H	2B	3B	HR	RBI	BB	SO	SB
19 Years	.287	2729	10,554	1570	3025	558	123	243	1355	922	1257	262
(Through 1992)												

GEORGE BRETT

Born: May 15, 1953, at Glen Dale, WV

Playing Career: Kansas City Royals (AL) 1973-Present

One of the greatest pure hitters to ever play the game ...The Kansas City Royals all-time leader in every offensive category ... Has led the American League in average (three times), hits (three times), total bases (twice), doubles (twice), triples (three times), on-base percentage and slugging percentage (three times) ... A 13-time All-Star, he has had 11 seasons with a .300 or better average and four seasons with 100 or more RBI ... Won AL batting crowns in 1976, 1980 and 1990, becoming the first player in history to win batting titles in three decades ... Hit .390 and posted a 30-game hitting streak in 1980 en route to being named the AL Most Valuable Player ... Became the 18th player in history to collect 3,000 career hits September 30, 1992, at California.

Playing Career	AVG	G	AB	R	H	2B	3B	HR	RBI	BB	SO	SB
20 Years	.307	2562	9789	1514	3005	634	134	298	1520	1057	840	194
(Through 1992)												

3,000 HIT CLUB

A Chronology

Name/Club	Date	Opponent	Pitcher	Hit Info
Cap Anson, Chgo	July 16, 1897	Baltimore	George Blackburn	Single
Honus Wagner, Pitt	June 9, 1914	Philadelphia	Erskine Mayer	Double
Nap Lajoie, Clev	Sept. 15, 1914	Detroit	Pug Cavet	Single
Ty Cobb, Det	August 19, 1921	Boston	Elmer Myers	Single
Tris Speaker, Cle	May 17, 1925	Washington	Tom Zachary	Single
Eddie Collins, CWS	June 6, 1925	Detroit	Walter Johnson	Double
Paul Waner, Bos	June 19, 1942	Pittsburgh	Rip Sewell	Single
Stan Musial, StL	May 13, 1958	Chgo Cubs	Moe Drabowsky	Double
Henry Aaron, Atl	May 17, 1970	Cincinnati	Wayne Simpson	Single
Willie Mays, SF	July 18, 1970	Montreal	Mike Wegener	Single
Roberto Clemente, Pitt	Sept. 30, 1972	NY Mets	Jon Matlack	Double
Al Kaline, Det	Sept. 24, 1974	Baltimore	Dave McNally	Double
Pete Rose, Phil	May 5, 1978	Montreal	Steve Rogers	Single
Lou Brock, StL	August 13, 1979	Chgo Cubs	Dennis Lamp	Single
Carl Yastrzemski, Bos	Sept. 12, 1979	NY Yankees	Jim Beattie	Single
Rod Carew, Cal	August 4, 1985	Minnesota	Frank Viola	Single
Robin Yount, Milw	Sept. 9, 1992	Cleveland	Jose Mesa	Single
George Brett, KC	Sept. 30, 1992	California	Tim Fortugno	Single
Dave Winfield, Minn	Sept. 16, 1993	Oakland	Dennis Eckersley	Single

Sources:
The Baseball Encyclopedia (Seventh Edition) edited by Joseph L. Reichler
The Baseball Chronology edited by James Charlton
The Baseball Hall Of Fame
The Ballplayers (First Edition) edited by Mike Shatzkin

Age Chart

Player	Date	Age	Career/Hits
Ty Cobb	August 19, 1921	34 Years, 8 Months, 01 Days	24 Yrs/4,191
Henry Aaron	May 17, 1970	36 Years, 3 Months, 12 Days	23 Yrs/3,771
Robin Yount	Sept. 9, 1992	36 Years, 11 Months, 24 Days	19 Yrs/3,132
Pete Rose	May 5, 1978	37 Years, 0 Months, 21 Days	24 Yrs/4,256
Tris Speaker	May 17, 1925	37 Years, 1 Months, 13 Days	22 Yrs/3,515
Stan Musial	May 13, 1958	37 Years, 5 Months, 22 Days	22 Yrs/3,630
Eddie Collins	June 6, 1925	38 Years, 1 Months, 01 Days	25 Yrs/3,311
Roberto Clemente	Sept. 30, 1972	38 Years, 1 Months, 12 Days	18 Yrs/3,000
Paul Waner	June 19, 1942	39 Years, 2 Months, 03 Days	20 Yrs/3,152
Willie Mays	July 18, 1970	39 Years, 2 Months, 12 Days	22 Yrs/3,283
George Brett	Sept. 30, 1992	39 Years, 4 Months, 15 Days	19 Yrs/3,137
Al Kaline	Sept. 24, 1974	39 Years, 9 Months, 05 Days	22 Yrs/3,007
Rod Carew	August 4, 1985	39 Years, 10 Months, 03 Days	19 Yrs/3,053
Carl Yastrzemski	Sept. 12, 1979	40 Years, 0 Months, 21 Days	23 Yrs/3,419
Honus Wagner	June 9, 1914	40 Years, 3 Months, 13 Days	21 Yrs/3,430
Nap Lajoie	Sept. 27, 1914	40 Years, 0 Months, 22 Days	21 Yrs/3,251
Lou Brock	August 13, 1979	40 Years, 1 Months, 25 Days	19 Yrs/3,023
Dave Winfield	Sept. 16. 1993	41 Years, 11 Months, 13 Days	20 Yrs/3,000
Cap Anson	July 18, 1897	46 Years, 2 Months, 07 Days	22 Yrs/3,041

▲ Dave Winfield with Rod Carew

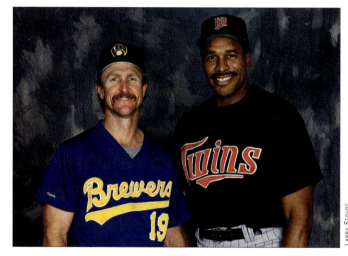

▲ Dave Winfield with Robin Yount

▲ Dave Winfield with George Brett

The Pitchers

Pitchers allowing hits to Dave Winfield, arranged in descending order.

PITCHER	HITS	1B	2B	3B	HR
Phil Niekro	32	22	8	0	2
Don Sutton	32	22	3	1	6
Jerry Koosman	25	14	4	0	7
Floyd Bannister	24	10	6	0	8
John Montefusco	23	16	5	0	2
Mike Flanagan	22	14	6	0	2
Frank Tanana	22	13	5	0	4
Bruce Hurst	20	10	5	1	4
Dan Petry	20	9	6	0	5
Dave Stieb	20	14	5	0	1
Bill Bonham	19	16	1	2	0
Steve Carlton	19	11	4	2	2
Roger Clemens	19	12	3	1	3
Ray Burris	18	15	1	1	1
Charlie Hough	18	8	4	0	6
Jimmy Key	18	13	3	1	1
Charlie Leibrandt	18	12	2	0	4
Mike Moore	18	13	1	1	3
Jack Morris	18	11	3	0	4
Tom Seaver	18	13	2	0	3
Jerry Reuss	17	13	2	0	2
Frank Viola	17	8	1	1	7
Doyle Alexander	16	12	3	1	0
Mike Caldwell	16	14	1	0	1
Craig Swan	16	11	1	2	2
Walt Terrell	16	14	1	0	1
Danny Darwin	15	9	2	0	4
Doug Rau	15	10	2	1	2
Rick Reuschel	15	11	4	0	0
J.R. Richard	15	12	3	0	0
Rick Sutcliffe	15	7	3	0	5
Jim Barr	14	10	3	1	0
Oil Can Boyd	14	4	8	0	2
John Cerutti	14	8	2	0	4
Ted Higuera	14	7	4	1	2
Tommy John	14	8	4	1	1
Jon Matlack	14	7	4	1	2
Rick Rhoden	14	8	2	0	4
Steve Rogers	14	12	1	0	1
Bob Forsch	13	8	2	1	2
Burt Hooton	13	6	4	0	3
Scott McGregor	13	9	3	0	1
Fred Norman	13	9	3	0	1
Jim Rooker	13	9	2	0	2
Joaquin Andujar	12	9	0	0	3
Bert Blyleven	12	6	2	0	4
Mike Boddicker	12	9	1	0	2
Jim Clancy	12	5	3	0	4
Bryan Clark	12	10	0	1	1
John Denny	12	8	3	0	1
Ken Forsch	12	9	1	0	2
Bob Kneppe	12	6	1	1	4
Joe Niekro	12	8	3	1	0
Scott Sanderson	12	7	3	1	1
Matt Young	12	5	2	0	5
Bud Black	11	7	1	0	3
Vida Blue	11	8	2	0	1
John Candelaria	11	8	1	0	2
Mark Gubicza	11	8	2	1	0
Dennis Martinez	11	6	3	1	1
Lynn McGlothen	11	7	2	2	0
Jaime Navarro	11	5	2	0	4
Gene Nelson	11	5	3	0	3
Dick Ruthven	11	5	3	2	1
Kevin Brown	10	6	0	0	4
Steve Crawford	10	5	2	2	1
Dennis Eckersley	10	7	3	0	0
Nino Espinosa	10	6	2	0	2
Chuck Finley	10	5	1	0	4
Woodie Fryman	10	10	0	0	0
Ross Grimsley	10	5	2	0	3
Rick Honeycutt	10	6	2	0	2
Jim Kaat	10	5	4	0	1
Dennis Lamp	10	5	3	1	1
Mark Langston	10	8	0	1	1
Ken Schrom	10	7	2	0	1
Mike Smithson	10	6	4	0	0
Dave Stewart	10	9	1	0	0
Pete Vuckovich	10	6	3	0	1
Bill Wegman	10	7	2	0	1

PITCHER	HITS	1B	2B	3B	HR
Bob Welch	10	7	1	0	2
David Wells	10	6	1	0	3
Ed Whitson	10	4	2	1	3
Scott Bankhead	9	3	4	0	2
Jack Billingham	9	9	0	0	0
Bill Caudill	9	6	1	0	2
Chris Codiroli	9	6	3	0	0
John Curtis	9	6	1	0	2
Lee Guetterman	9	7	0	1	1
Bill Gullickson	9	8	1	0	0
Larry Gura	9	7	0	1	1
Greg Hibbard	9	6	1	0	2
LaMarr Hoyt	9	5	3	0	1
Ben.McDonald	9	3	4	0	2
Carl Morton.	9	5	0	2	2
Bob Ojeda	9	5	3	1	0
Ron Reed	9	7	1	0	1
Bret Saberhagen	9	6	2	1	0
Elias Sosa	9	3	4	0	2
Dan Spillner	9	5	2	0	2
Tom Underwood	9	8	0	0	1
Juan Berenguer	8	5	2	0	1
Chris Bosio	8	4	1	0	3
Tom Candiotti	8	8	0	0	0
John Habyan	8	5	3	0	0
Ed Halicki	8	5	2	1	0
Erik Hanson	8	3	4	0	1
Brad Havens	8	4	3	0	1
Danny Jackson	8	5	2	0	1
Bill Krueger	8	6	2	0	0
Gary Lavelle	8	7	0	0	1
Kirk McCaskill	8	7	1	0	0
Steve McCatty	8	3	3	2	0
Dave A.Roberts	8	5	0	0	3
Ron Romanick	8	5	1	0	2
Sammy Stewart	8	4	1	1	2
Bruce Sutter	8	5	3	0	0
Bill Swift	8	6	1	0	1
Bobby Witt	8	7	0	0	1
Curt Young	8	3	2	0	3
Geoff Zahn	8	4	2	0	2
Jim Abbott	7	7	0	0	0
Mark Clear	7	3	3	0	1
John D'Acquisto	7	5	1	0	1
Ken Dixon	7	2	1	0	4
Richard Dotson	7	3	2	1	1
Jamie Easterly	7	4	0	0	3
Roric Harrison	7	5	1	0	1
Randy Johnson	7	1	3	1	2
Dave LaPoint	7	6	1	0	0
Randy Lerch	7	3	1	1	2
Mickey Mahler	7	3	1	2	1
Tippy Martinez	7	5	0	1	1
Bo McLaughlin	7	6	1	0	0
Larry McWilliams	7	4	1	1	1
Juan Nieves	7	4	1	0	2
Al Nipper	7	4	2	1	0
Gaylord Perry	7	3	1	0	3
Jeff Russell	7	4	3	0	0
Jim Slaton	7	4	2	0	1
Lary Sorensen	7	5	2	0	0
Don Stanhouse	7	6	0	0	1
Mike T.Stanton	7	5	1	0	1
Greg Swindell	7	3	1	0	3
Kevin Tapani	7	6	0	0	1
John Tudor	7	4	0	0	3
Wayne Twitchell	7	5	1	0	1
Al Williams	7	4	1	2	0
Don Aase	6	4	2	0	0
Jim Acker	6	4	0	0	2
DougBair	6	3	2	0	1
Jeff Ballard	6	6	0	0	0
Jim Bibby	6	5	1	0	0
Tommy Boggs	6	5	1	0	0
Pedro Borbon	6	5	1	0	0
Britt Burns	6	4	1	1	0
Greg Cadaret	6	4	2	0	0
Chuck Crim	6	5	0	0	1
Storm Davis	6	6	0	0	0
Larry Demery	6	4	1	0	1

PITCHER	HITS	1B	2B	3B	HR
Willie Fraser	6	3	0	0	3
Rich Gale	6	4	1	1	0
Mike Garman	6	5	0	0	1
Jerry Don Gleaton	6	4	1	0	1
Tom Gordon	6	4	0	0	2
Don Gullett	6	5	0	0	1
Preston Hanna	6	4	1	0	1
Greg A. Harris	6	4	1	0	1
Neal Heaton	6	3	0	0	3
Tom Hume	6	5	1	0	0
Rick Langford	6	3	1	0	2
Tim Leary	6	4	2	0	0
Jack McDowell	6	3	1	0	2
Andy Messersmith	6	4	2	0	0
Mike Mussina	6	1	3	0	2
Claude Osteen	6	4	2	0	0
Larry Pashnick	6	5	0	0	1
Eric Plunk	6	3	2	0	1
Paul Splittorff	6	3	1	0	2
Bob Stanley	6	5	1	0	0
Steve Stone	6	6	0	0	0
BobbyThigpen	6	4	0	0	2
Rick Waits	6	4	0	0	2
Carl Willis	6	4	2	0	0
Mike Witt	6	5	0	1	0
Santo Alcala	5	3	2	0	0
Luis Aquino	5	4	1	0	0
Keith Atherton	5	4	0	0	1
Jim Beattie	5	3	1	0	1
Eric Bell	5	3	1	0	1
DeWayne Buice	5	3	0	0	2
Rick Camp	5	4	1	0	0
Larry Christenson	5	2	1	0	2
Steve Comer	5	4	0	0	1
Al Downing	5	4	1	0	0
Pete Falcone	5	3	1	0	1
Jose Guzman	5	3	0	0	2
Doug Henry	5	4	0	0	1
Willie Hernandez	5	4	0	1	0
Joe Hesketh	5	1	3	0	1
Mike Jeffcoat	5	4	1	0	0
Doug Jones	5	4	1	0	0
Odell Jones	5	3	0	2	0
Doug Konieczny	5	5	0	0	0
Mike Krukow	5	4	0	1	0
Luis Leal	5	3	1	0	1
Mark Lemongello	5	2	1	0	2
Jim Lonborg	5	2	2	1	0
Aurelio Lopez	5	4	0	0	1
Mike Mason	5	5	0	0	0
Rick Matula	5	4	0	0	1
Donnie Moore	5	2	1	0	2
Dale Murray	5	4	0	1	0
Charles Nagy	5	3	1	1	0
Rod Nichols	5	4	1	0	0
Gary Nolan	5	2	1	0	2
Edwin Nunez	5	5	0	0	0
Jim Palmer	5	3	0	0	2
Frank Pastore	5	4	1	0	0
Melido Perez	5	3	1	0	1
Steve Renko	5	4	0	0	1
Jeff M Robinson	5	3	2	0	0
Vern Ruhle	5	4	1	0	0
Dave Schmidt	5	5	0	0	0
Hector Wagner	5	2	1	0	2
Dan Warthen	5	3	1	0	1
Pat Zachry	5	2	2	0	1
Neil Allen	4	4	0	0	0
Allan Anderson	4	4	0	0	0
Bud Anderson	4	2	1	0	1
Scott Bailes	4	1	2	0	1
Dave Beard	4	3	0	0	1
Ricky Bones	4	4	0	0	0
Ken Brett	4	2	1	0	1
John Butcher	4	2	2	0	0
Dave Campbell	4	3	0	0	1
Edwin Correa	4	1	1	0	2
John Dopson	4	3	0	0	1
Rob Dressler	4	4	0	0	0
Rawley Eastwick	4	3	1	0	0

PITCHER	HITS	1B	2B	3B	HR
Dock Ellis	4	3	1	0	0
Alex Fernandez	4	3	1	0	0
Gene Garber	4	3	0	0	1
Mike Gardiner	4	2	2	0	0
Dave Goltz	4	2	1	0	1
DaveGumpert	4	4	0	0	0
Tom Henke	4	2	0	0	2
John Henry Johnson	4	2	2	0	0
Scott Kamieniecki	4	3	1	0	0
Paul Kilgus	4	4	0	0	0
Clay Kirby	4	2	1	0	1
Bruce Kison	4	4	0	0	0
Mike LaCoss	4	4	0	0	0
Skip Lockwood	4	3	0	0	1
Bob McClure	4	1	1	0	2
Jose Mesa	4	4	0	0	0
Jack O'Connor	4	4	0	0	0
Steve Ontiveros	4	3	1	0	0
Donn Pall	4	4	0	0	0
Dan Quisenberry	4	4	0	0	0
Dave Rozema	4	4	0	0	0
Joe Sambito	4	3	1	0	0
Roy Smith	4	3	0	0	1
George Stone	4	3	0	0	1
Randy Tate	4	2	2	0	0
Kent Tekulve	4	2	0	0	2
Dave Tobik	4	2	2	0	0
Rick Williams	4	3	1	0	0
Frank Wills	4	2	0	0	2
Paul Abbott	3	3	0	0	0
Kevin Appier	3	3	0	0	0
Mike Armstrong	3	1	0	1	1
Bill Atkinson	3	3	0	0	0
Jerry Augustine	3	1	1	0	1
Howard Bailey	3	2	0	0	1
Len Barker	3	3	0	0	0
Salome Barojas	3	1	1	0	1
Karl Best	3	1	1	0	1
Tom Bolton	3	3	0	0	0
Mark Bomback	3	3	0	0	0
Tom Bradley	3	1	2	0	0
Tony Brizzolara	3	2	0	0	1
Todd Burns	3	1	1	1	0
Doug Capilla	3	3	0	0	0
Don Carrithers	3	2	1	0	0
Clay Carroll	3	3	0	0	0
Bobby Castillo	3	1	1	0	1
Terry Clark	3	1	1	0	1
Jaime Cocanower	3	2	0	0	1
Mike Cosgrove	3	2	1	0	0
Bruce Dal Canton	3	3	0	0	0
Ron Darling	3	3	0	0	0
Joel Davis	3	2	1	0	0
Rich DeLucia	3	1	1	0	1
Adrian Devine	3	2	0	0	1
Tom Dixon	3	2	1	0	0
Tom Edens	3	3	0	0	0
Mark Eichhorn	3	2	1	0	0
Steve Farr	3	3	0	0	0
Dave Frost	3	3	0	0	0
Mark Gardner	3	0	2	0	1
Dave Giusti	3	2	0	0	1
Tom Griffin	3	2	1	0	0
Dave Heaverlo	3	3	0	0	0
Don Hood	3	2	0	0	1
Roy Lee Jackson	3	1	1	0	1
Matt Keough	3	2	1	0	0
Eric King	3	3	0	0	0
Kevin Kobel	3	2	0	0	1
Frank LaCorte	3	3	0	0	0
Dan Larson	3	2	0	0	1
Charlie Lea	3	2	1	0	0
Terry Leach	3	1	1	0	1
Bill Lee	3	2	1	0	0
Mark Leiter	3	3	0	0	0
Max Leon	3	1	0	0	2
Dennis Leonard	3	1	1	0	1
Mickey Lolich	3	1	2	0	0
Mike Marshall	3	2	0	0	1
Silvio Martinez	3	3	0	0	0

PITCHER	HITS	1B	2B	3B	HR
Terry Mathews	3	2	1	0	0
Tug McGraw	3	1	1	0	1
Doc Medich	3	2	0	1	0
Greg Minton	3	3	0	0	0
Randy Moffitt	3	2	1	0	0
Mike Morgan	3	3	0	0	0
Paul Moskau	3	2	1	0	0
Jamie Moyer	3	0	2	1	0
Randy Niemann	3	3	0	0	0
Dickie Noles	3	2	0	0	1
Dan Plesac	3	1	1	0	0
Dennis Powell	3	1	2	0	0
Ted Power	3	3	0	0	0
Rick Reed	3	2	0	0	1
Nolan Ryan	3	3	0	0	0
Manny Sarmiento	3	3	0	0	0
Dan Schatzeder	3	1	2	0	0
Calvin Schiraldi	3	2	0	0	1
Mike Schooler	3	2	0	0	1
Ron Schueler	3	1	0	1	1
Don Schulze	3	3	0	0	0
Aaron Sele	3	2	1	0	0
Eddie Solomon	3	1	1	0	1
Tom Tellmann	3	2	0	0	1
Roy Thomas	3	1	1	1	0
Mark Thurmond	3	2	0	0	1
Dave Tomlin	3	3	0	0	0
Mike Torrez	3	2	1	0	0
Steve Trout	3	3	0	0	0
Julio Valera	3	1	1	0	1
Ed VandeBerg	3	1	1	0	1
Curt Wardle	3	0	0	0	3
Charlie Williams	3	2	0	0	1
Juan Agosto	2	2	0	0	0
Jay Aldrich	2	1	0	0	1
Gerald Alexander	2	2	0	0	0
Rick Anderson	2	1	1	0	0
Bob Apodaca	2	2	0	0	0
Brad Arnsberg	2	1	1	0	0
Don August	2	1	1	0	0
Rick Baldwin	2	1	1	0	0
John Barfield	2	1	1	0	0
Mike Beard	2	2	0	0	0
Sean Bergman	2	2	0	0	0
Mike Bielecki	2	2	0	0	0
Brian Bohanon	2	1	0	0	1
Jim Brewer	2	2	0	0	0
Mark Brown	2	2	0	0	0
Jackie Brown	2	2	0	0	0
Ernie Camacho	2	2	0	0	0
Mike Campbell	2	0	1	0	1
Chuck Cary	2	0	1	1	0
Larry Casian	2	1	0	0	1
Scott Chiamparino	2	2	0	0	0
Steve Chitren	2	2	0	0	0
Tim Conroy	2	1	0	0	1
Dennis Cook	2	2	0	0	0
Jim Crawford	2	2	0	0	0
Mike Dalton	2	1	0	0	1
Ron Davis	2	2	0	0	0
Don DeMola	2	1	1	0	0
Jerry DiPoto	2	1	1	0	0
Tim Drummond	2	2	0	0	0
Wayne Edwards	2	1	1	0	0
Cal Eldred	2	2	0	0	0
John Farrell	2	2	0	0	0
Rollie Fingers	2	2	0	0	0
Brian Fisher	2	2	0	0	0
Ken Frailing	2	0	0	0	2
Todd Frohwirth	2	0	1	0	1
Wes Gardner	2	1	1	0	0
Wayne Garland	2	1	0	0	1
Bob L. Gibson	2	2	0	0	0
Bob Gibson	2	1	0	0	1
Don Gordon	2	1	1	0	0
Jim Gott	2	2	0	0	0
Joe Grahe	2	1	0	0	1
Mark Guthrie	2	0	0	0	2
Moose Haas	2	1	0	0	1
Tom Hall	2	1	0	0	1
Dave Hamilton	2	1	1	0	0
Atlee Hammaker	2	1	1	0	0
Gerald Hannahs	2	1	0	0	1
Steve Hargan	2	1	0	0	1
Pete Harnisch	2	2	0	0	0
Andy Hassler	2	2	0	0	0
Tom Hausman	2	0	0	0	2
Andy Hawkins	2	1	0	0	1
Kevin Hickey	2	2	0	0	0
Shawn Hillegas	2	2	0	0	0
Ken Holtzman	2	1	0	0	1

PITCHER	HITS	1B	2B	3B	HR
Steve Howe	2	1	1	0	0
Jay Howell	2	0	2	0	0
Grant Jackson	2	1	1	0	0
Bob James	2	1	1	0	0
Jesse Jefferson	2	1	1	0	0
Jeff Jones	2	1	1	0	0
Mike Jones	2	0	1	1	0
Joe Kerrigan	2	0	1	1	0
Brian Kingman	2	1	0	1	0
Kurt Knudsen	2	1	1	0	0
Lew Krausse	2	2	0	0	0
Lerrin LaGrow	2	1	0	0	1
Dennis Lewallyn	2	2	0	0	0
Graeme Lloyd	2	2	0	0	0
Bill Long	2	2	0	0	0
Rick Lysander	2	2	0	0	0
Mike Magnante	2	2	0	0	0
Pat Mahomes	2	1	1	0	0
Juan Marichal	2	2	0	0	0
Ernie McAnally	2	1	1	0	0
Joey McLaughlin	2	2	0	0	0
Dave McNally	2	2	0	0	0
Bob Miller	2	2	0	0	0
John Mitchell	2	1	1	0	0
Jeff Montgomery	2	2	0	0	0
Jeff Musselman	2	2	0	0	0
Mike Norris	2	2	0	0	0
John Odom	2	2	0	0	0
Steve Olin	2	2	0	0	0
Randy O'Neal	2	2	0	0	0
Dave Otto	2	1	0	0	1
David Palmer	2	1	0	0	1
Jon Perlman	2	1	1	0	0
Joe Price	2	1	0	0	1
Paul Quantrill	2	2	0	0	0
Scott Radinsky	2	1	1	0	0
Paul Reuschel	2	2	0	0	0
Allen Ripley	2	1	0	0	1
Bert Roberge	2	2	0	0	0
Ron Robinson	2	1	1	0	0
Enrique Romo	2	1	0	0	1
Jeff Shaw	2	1	1	0	0
Sonny Siebert	2	1	1	0	0
Mark Smith	2	1	1	0	0
Mario Soto	2	2	0	0	0
Todd Stottlemyre	2	2	0	0	0
Bill Swaggerty	2	2	0	0	0
Russ Swan	2	1	0	0	1
Mike Timlin	2	0	1	0	1
Tom Waddell	2	2	0	0	0
Bob Walk	2	2	0	0	0
Stan Wall	2	0	1	0	1
Dave Wallace	2	1	0	0	1
Chris Welch	2	2	0	0	0
Bob Wickman	2	1	1	0	0
Mark Williamson	2	2	0	0	0
Rich Yett	2	1	0	0	1
Brian Allard	1	0	0	0	1
Luis Aponte	1	1	0	0	0
Jack Armstrong	1	1	0	0	0
Tony Arnold	1	0	1	0	0
James Austin	1	1	0	0	0
Stan Bahnsen	1	1	0	0	0
Dick Baney	1	1	0	0	0
Rich Barnes	1	1	0	0	0
Ross Baumgarten	1	0	1	0	0
Jose Bautista	1	1	0	0	0
Joe Beckwith	1	1	0	0	0
Tim Belcher	1	0	1	0	0
Dwight Bernard	1	0	0	0	1
Doug Bird	1	1	0	0	0
Mike Birkbeck	1	1	0	0	0
Joe Bitker	1	0	1	0	0
Jeff Bittiger	1	1	0	0	0
Rich Bordi	1	1	0	0	0
Tom Brennan	1	0	0	0	1
Pete Broberg	1	1	0	0	0
Mike Brown	1	0	1	0	0
Warren Brusstar	1	1	0	0	0
Tom Burgmeier	1	0	1	0	0
George Capuzzello	1	1	0	0	0
Tom Carroll	1	0	1	0	0
Bill Castro	1	1	0	0	0
Norm Charlton	1	1	0	0	0
Mark Clark	1	1	0	0	0
Pat Clements	1	1	0	0	0
Bryan Clutterbuck	1	1	0	0	0
Glen Cook	1	0	0	0	1
Don Cooper	1	1	0	0	0
Doug Corbett	1	1	0	0	0
Sherman Corbett	1	0	1	0	0

PITCHER	HITS	1B	2B	3B	HR
Joe Cowley	1	0	1	0	0
Danny Cox	1	1	0	0	0
Mark Davis	1	0	0	0	1
John Davis	1	1	0	0	0
Ken Dayley	1	1	0	0	0
Jeff Dedmon	1	1	0	0	0
Jose DeLeon	1	1	0	0	0
Tom Dettore	1	1	0	0	0
Larry Dierker	1	0	1	0	0
John Doherty	1	0	1	0	0
Kelly Downs	1	1	0	0	0
Dick Drago	1	1	0	0	0
Brian Drahman	1	1	0	0	0
Hal Dues	1	0	0	1	0
Steve Dunning	1	0	0	1	0
Bruce Egloff	1	1	0	0	0
Alan Embree	1	0	0	0	1
Scott Erickson	1	1	0	0	0
Bob Fallon	1	1	0	0	0
Ed Farmer	1	1	0	0	0
Mike Fetters	1	1	0	0	0
Pete Filson	1	0	1	0	0
Dave Fleming	1	0	1	0	0
Terry Forster	1	1	0	0	0
Alan Foster	1	1	0	0	0
Jimmy Freeman	1	1	0	0	0
Danny Frisella	1	1	0	0	0
John Fulgham	1	1	0	0	0
Dan Gakeler	1	1	0	0	0
Gary Gentry	1	0	0	0	1
Paul Gibson	1	0	1	0	0
Ed Glynn	1	1	0	0	0
German Gonzalez	1	1	0	0	0
Jeff Gray	1	1	0	0	0
Mike Griffin	1	0	0	0	1
Juan Guzman	1	1	0	0	0
Mike Hampton	1	1	0	0	0
Chris Haney	1	1	0	0	0
Reggie Harris	1	0	0	0	1
Gorman Heimueller	1	1	0	0	0
Don Heinkel	1	1	0	0	0
Mike Henneman	1	1	0	0	0
Dwayne Henry	1	0	1	0	0
Jesus Hernaiz	1	0	0	0	1
Ramon Hernandez	1	0	0	0	1
Roberto Hernandez	1	1	0	0	0
Fred Holdsworth	1	1	0	0	0
Al Holland	1	0	0	1	0
Brad Holman	1	1	0	0	0
Brian Holman	1	1	0	0	0
Darren Holmes	1	1	0	0	0
Ricky Horton	1	1	0	0	0
Tom House	1	1	0	0	0
Al Hrabosky	1	1	0	0	0
Mark Huismann	1	1	0	0	0
Mike Ignasiak	1	0	0	0	1
Darrell Jackson	1	0	1	0	0
Curt Kaufman	1	1	0	0	0
Bryan Kelly	1	1	0	0	0
Jim Kern	1	0	1	0	0
Tom Klawitter	1	0	0	0	1
Joe Klink	1	1	0	0	0
Mark Knudson	1	1	0	0	0
Bob Lacey	1	1	0	0	0
Pete Ladd	1	0	1	0	0
Bob Lang	1	1	0	0	0
Jack Lazorko	1	1	0	0	0
Dave Leiper	1	0	0	0	1
Mark Littell	1	1	0	0	0
Tim Lollar	1	1	0	0	0
Steve Luebber	1	1	0	0	0
Julio Machado	1	1	0	0	0
John Martin	1	0	1	0	0
Matt Maysey	1	0	0	0	1
Will McEnaney	1	1	0	0	0
Andy McGaffigan	1	1	0	0	0
Joel McKeon	1	0	0	0	1
Craig McMurtry	1	0	0	1	0
Butch Metzger	1	1	0	0	0
Bob Milacki	1	0	1	0	0
Dyar Miller	1	0	0	0	1
Charlie Mitchell	1	1	0	0	0
Dale Mohorcic	1	1	0	0	0
John Montague	1	1	0	0	0
Rich Monteleone	1	1	0	0	0
Bill Mooneyham	1	1	0	0	0
Balor Moore	1	1	0	0	0
Bob Moose	1	1	0	0	0
Roger Moret	1	1	0	0	0
John Morlan	1	0	0	1	0
Kevin Morton	1	0	0	0	1

PITCHER	HITS	1B	2B	3B	HR
Bobby Munoz	1	1	0	0	0
Mike Munoz	1	1	0	0	0
Steve Mura	1	1	0	0	0
Tom Murphy	1	0	1	0	0
Ron Musselman	1	1	0	0	0
Jeff Mutis	1	0	1	0	0
Bob Myrick	1	0	0	1	0
Roger Nelson	1	1	0	0	0
Jeff Nelson	1	1	0	0	0
Scott Nielsen	1	1	0	0	0
Gregg Olson	1	1	0	0	0
Jesse Orosco	1	1	0	0	0
Bob Owchinko	1	0	0	0	1
John Pacella	1	1	0	0	0
Harry Parker	1	0	1	0	0
Clay Parker	1	0	0	0	1
Ken Patterson	1	1	0	0	0
Dave Patterson	1	0	0	0	1
Roger Pavlik	1	1	0	0	0
John Pawlowski	1	1	0	0	0
Bill Pecota	1	0	0	1	0
Gene Pentz	1	0	0	0	1
Horacio Pina	1	1	0	0	0
Mark Portugal	1	0	1	0	0
Chuck Rainey	1	1	0	0	0
Eric Rasmussen	1	1	0	0	0
Jeff Reardon	1	1	0	0	0
Pete Redfern	1	1	0	0	0
Jerry Reed	1	0	1	0	0
Arthur Rhodes	1	1	0	0	0
Don A Robinson	1	1	0	0	0
Kenny Rogers	1	1	0	0	0
Jose Roman	1	1	0	0	0
Mike Rowland	1	0	1	0	0
Bruce Ruffin	1	0	1	0	0
Ray Sadecki	1	1	0	0	0
Kevin Saucier	1	1	0	0	0
Mac Scarce	1	1	0	0	0
Jeff Schneider	1	0	0	0	1
Buddy Schultz	1	0	0	0	1
Scott Scudder	1	1	0	0	0
Rudy Seanez	1	0	1	0	0
Ray Searage	1	1	0	0	0
Greg Shanahan	1	1	0	0	0
Doug Sisk	1	1	0	0	0
Joe Slusarski	1	0	1	0	0
John Smiley	1	1	0	0	0
Lee Smith	1	1	0	0	0
Dave Smith	1	1	0	0	0
Nate Snell	1	0	0	0	1
Russ Springer	1	0	0	0	1
Rick Steirer	1	1	0	0	0
Bob Stoddard	1	1	0	0	0
Les Straker	1	1	0	0	0
John Strohmayer	1	0	0	0	1
Bob Sykes	1	0	1	0	0
Chuck Taylor	1	0	1	0	0
Terry Taylor	1	0	1	0	0
Jeff Terpko	1	1	0	0	0
Duane Theiss	1	0	1	0	0
Mike Thompson	1	1	0	0	0
Dick Tidrow	1	1	0	0	0
Jackson Todd	1	0	1	0	0
Fred Toliver	1	1	0	0	0
Bill Travers	1	0	1	0	0
Mike Trombley	1	0	1	0	0
Jerry Ujdur	1	1	0	0	0
Pat Underwood	1	1	0	0	0
John Urrea	1	1	0	0	0
Fernando Valenzuela	1	1	0	0	0
Todd Van Poppel	1	1	0	0	0
DeWayne Vaughn	1	1	0	0	0
Mike Walker	1	0	1	0	0
Tom Walker	1	1	0	0	0
Duane Ward	1	1	0	0	0
Gary Wayne	1	1	0	0	0
David West	1	0	0	0	1
Len Whitehouse	1	0	0	1	0
Matt Whiteside	1	1	0	0	0
Milt Wilcox	1	1	0	0	0
Bill Wilkinson	1	1	0	0	0
Dick Williams	1	1	0	0	0
Matt Williams	1	0	0	0	1
Mitch Williams	1	0	1	0	0
Jim Winn	1	1	0	0	0
Bob Woodward	1	1	0	0	0
Jim York	1	1	0	0	0
Oscar Zamora	1	0	0	0	1